Woodland Crafting

Patrick Harrison

Hawthorn Press

Woodland Crafting © 2023 Patrick Harrison

Patrick Harrison is hereby identified as the author of this work in accordance with section 77 of the Copyright, Designs and Patent Act, 1988. He asserts and gives notice of his moral right under this Act.

Published by Hawthorn Press, Hawthorn House, 1 Lansdown Lane, Stroud, Gloucestershire, GL5 1BJ, UK Tel: 01453 757040   Email: info@hawthornpress.com   Website: www.hawthornpress.com

Hawthorn Press

All rights reserved. It is permissible for the purchaser to make the projects contained herein solely for personal use. No other part of this book may be reproduced or utilised in any form or by any means including photocopying, recording or by any electronic or mechanical means including information storage and retrieval systems without prior permission in writing from the publisher.

Illustrations by Patrick Harrison
Cover design and typesetting by Lucy Guenot
Printed 2023 by Short Run Press Ltd, Exeter, UK
Printed on environmentally friendly paper manufactured from renewable forest stock.

Previously published under the title Making Woodland Crafts ISBN: 978-1-907359-84-2
Every effort has been made to trace the ownership of all copyrighted material. If any omission has been made, please bring this to the publisher's attention so that proper acknowledgement may be given in future editions.

The views expressed in this book are not necessarily those of the publisher.
British Library Cataloguing in Publication Data applied for
ISBN 978-1-912480-83-8

Photography credits:
Page 16 (below) Wikimedia
Other photography by Lucy Guenot

Woodland Crafting

Patrick Harrison

30 projects for children

Hawthorn Press

Contents

Foreword by David Bond		6
Introduction by Patrick Harrison		8
How to use this book		10
Useful tools		11
Choosing your wood		12
Hazel		13
Willow		14
Birch		15
Elder		16
Some useful knots and lashings		17
Overhand knot		18
Clove hitch		19
Square lashing		20
Sheer lashing		22
Whipping		23
Netting		25
Things to make		27
Hazel mask		28
Festive candle		30
Mini hurdle		32
French arrow		34
Night torch		37
Dead hedging		39
Staff		40
Making and mending tools		43
Making frames and simple structures		45
Nature picture		46
Ladder		48
Stretcher		49
Star gazer		50

The tripod	54
Making a tripod	55
Tripod seat	57
Tripod monsters	58
The triangle	59
Making a triangle	60
Modular triangles	61
Tetrahedron	62
Step ladder	63
Lantern	64
Fixing a tea light inside your lantern	65
Using elder and willow	66
Blow pipe	67
Elder beads	69
Forest rosaries	70
Preparing willow cordage	71
Macramé bracelet 1	74
Macramé bracelet 2	75
Macramé bracelet 3	77

Making puppets	81
Simple elder bead puppet	82
Horse puppet	84
Man of the forest puppet	87
Giant puppets	90
Giant horse puppet	91
Giant dragon puppet	92
Afterword by Jon Cree	94

Foreword

Inspirational teachers spark our interest in a subject and can ignite a passion for life. For Roger Deakin, author of *Waterlog* and *Wildwood*, it was Barry Goater, his sixth form biology teacher. Goater would take his class on camping trips to the New Forest, where they'd study the botany, zoology and ecology of the area. It was where Deakin learnt the 'intimate kinship of ecology and poetry' that features throughout his writing.

Patrick Harrison is another of these inspirational teachers. Not just that, but he is the teacher from whom other teachers learn. I have had the pleasure of watching Patrick teach. He is as assured, diligent and kind with the children who come to his forest school sessions as he is with the forest school teachers who come to his sessions to learn. Patrick is the teachers' teacher.

This wonderful book shouts Patrick's passion for woodland craft. For him, as for many people, there is something about working in and with nature that is instantly accessible and easy. However, learning in classrooms or working in offices does not come so easily. This is not something I used to understand. I used to be a teacher, so was happy in classrooms. Offices did not bother me. Until, that is, several years ago, when I found myself in broadleaf woodland deep in the heart of Sussex, filming a group of teenage boys for my feature documentary *Project Wild Thing*. There was an overwhelming sense of calm. The children became lost in the atmosphere of the wood. I asked the boys what they loved about their surroundings. 'Freedom and peace', they replied. For them the woods are almost a spiritual haven, connecting them to nature.

So it was for John Muir, the Scottish-American conservationist. 'I only went out for a walk and finally concluded to stay out till sundown', he scribbled in his journal. 'For going out, I found, was really going in.' Nature is the ultimate remedy, comfort blanket, place to learn and backdrop to discovery.

When my daughter, Ivy, started attending Forest School sessions she came home with a glow in her eyes and a new story to tell. I used to be the one dragging my children out and encouraging them to take an interest in the nature around them. Now they lead the walks and stop to listen to birdcalls.

This book is not simply a feast for the eye and the soul, but for the imagination too. Every new page will lead you outdoors to forage, collect, make and do. Patrick's book is for anyone who teaches at a forest school or who knows a child who goes to one. It is for anyone who wants to tie the perfect clove hitch knot or create the ultimate den. This is the book for the budding Swallow or Amazon. And we need more Swallows and Amazons. Children in the UK have never been so disconnected from nature. It damages their health and wellbeing – and potentially the health of the planet too.

The skills *Woodland Crafting* teaches are not luxuries. They are not the product of middle-class technophobia. They are an important link to a more sustainable way of living. Patrick gives young people the tools to get outdoors and make their own adventures. That is a very good thing.

David Bond
Founder of *The Wild Network* and filmmaker of 'Project Wild Thing'

Introduction

When I was four my family went on holiday to Ireland. With seven of us crammed into a VW campervan long before it was deemed to be cool to own one, there were, inevitably, frequent arguments. It was after one of these lengthy altercations that my family noticed that I was not there anymore. After an hour of searching they found me sitting under a tree beside a small pond. I had found my antidote to chaos. One which, when required, I have resorted to as a matter of course since then. It fascinates me that so many others also seek out woodland as a calming oasis when overwhelmed by the madness of this world. And since then I have managed to make a living out of exploring the potential of this calming environment, predominantly as a context for learning. Anyone who has seen a group of children utterly lost to the world whilst absorbed in a woodland activity will know what I mean, a state called deep level learning, which has been scientifically proven to assist the release of a chemical called dopamine. A state that seems to assist the body and mind in exploring and absorbing the world around it.

This book has been assembled over many hundreds of hours spent messing about in the woods, hours that I am lucky enough to have been paid for as a Forest School practitioner and trainer. It is a book intended for anyone, of any age, with a modicum of interest. You may have ventured deep into the woods someplace, sometime before, or you may have never explored further than the back garden, or perhaps the outdoors is a completely new but enticing experience. It does not matter.

It will be very useful for parents who would like to take their own children out for an inspiring and creative day. It will also be extremely useful for teachers who would like some good ideas for excursions, and for outdoor learning practitioners who have dedicated their living to this massively rewarding field, perhaps awakened to the extraordinary beneficial scope for everyone, adults and children, involved in this process.

Why have I made this book in this particular way? Well, in truth, I've made it for me, and for those like me, who have gone through life a little bewildered and feeling inadequate. Simply because we do not necessarily absorb information the way other people do, either by listening to others conveying it through auditory instruction, or by trying to penetrate copious blocks of text, black on white. Information conveyed through dense, or even thin paragraphs, bullet points, and lists, for many of us, make our eyes sweat and our brains ache. In my case, it took a long time to understand that I had not been lazy, or stupid, as I was sometimes led to believe, at school. I had been just one of millions of others who do not absorb information that way. I am, as I eventually found out, a visual and kinaesthetic learner. I need big clear pictures. I need to see things as big and brash as possible in order to understand them. Over the years that I have delivered Outdoor Learning I have found this also to be true for hundreds of children and adults who I have had the privilege of working with.

What I offer, I hope, is within the ethos of Forest School, to promote the process of learning by offering various levels of achievability to match the current skills of your children.

I hope that the ideas in this book open doors to inspire your own creativity. I hope that you are urged to go beyond the projects described, using them as a springboard to create your own. If this book stimulates the process of thinking more creatively and spontaneously, then I could not hope for a better outcome.

My intention has been to provide a feast for the eye and soul, and to inspire and motivate others of all ages to get stuck in and explore the amazing woodland world of creativity.

Patrick Harrison

How to use this book

The book has been divided into sections intended to make it as practical to use as possible. Much of the skill of making the most of a woodland environment in a sustainable way is linked to knowing what you are using and whether it will renew itself. Knowing how each species behaves when used is also very important, and recognising whether green wood is knot free, for example, for ease of crafting in small hands. In reality this comes with practice, nevertheless I have included an introduction to some of the species used for the projects in this book to start you off.

There is also an introductory section about the tools you might need for the activities described, and a section on some useful knots and lashes which the book will refer you back to from time to time. I strongly suggest you learn the knots in the context of each activity rather than attempting them all at once before beginning the projects. They are so much more easily learnt when they are doing the job they were invented to do.

In fact the whole idea is to dip in and try out the projects that appeal rather than going through the book in the order it is presented. However, the sections flow with a perceived build up of understanding, within the ethos of Forest School, and that can be a powerful learning method. For example in the section on making triangles, I have first shown how to make a simple one. From there you can see what structures can be made from several of these, of which there are endless possibilities. I then suggest making a tetrahedron from three triangles as a 'doorway' to other possible structures, such as a very useful mobile step ladder. Having offered these useful structures in the book, however, I should stress that I always see what the children come up with through their own exploration first.

The challenge to adults brought up in a predominantly didactic learning environment (which I am not knocking – it certainly has its place) is to resist the urge to control things too much rather than allowing our young charges to find out what latent talents are hiding both in the depths of the woodland environment, and in the innate undergrowth of their own minds.

Useful tools

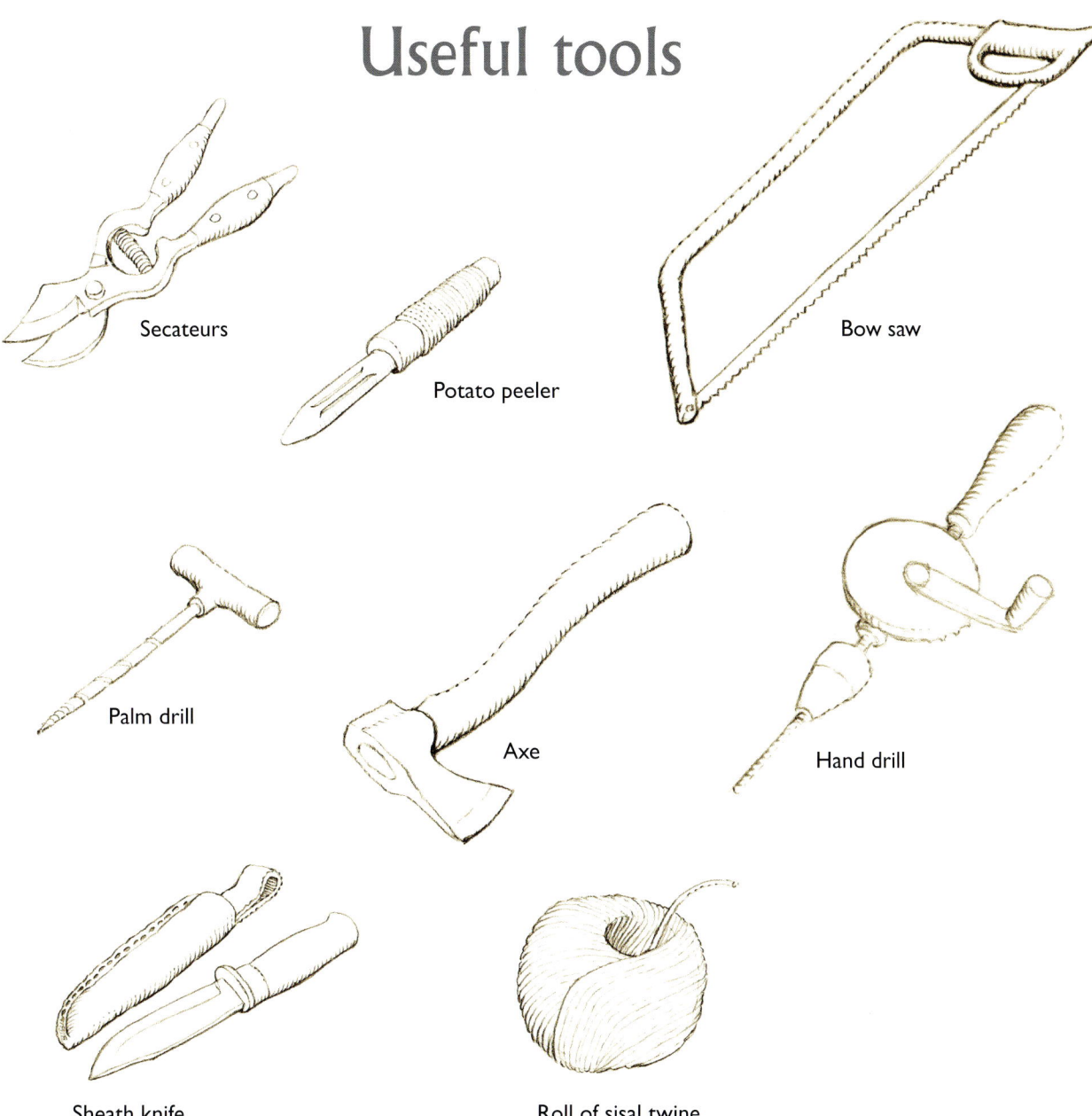

Choosing your wood

Learning about tree species helps build an understanding of the innate properties and qualities of different woods so that we can use them to maximum effect. For participants this can make all the difference in terms of the enjoyment and success of the projects they undertake.

Hazel

Hazel is an ideal choice of wood for many of the projects outlined in this book.

Hazel coppices have been nursed and sustained for hundreds of years in the United Kingdom in order to support traditional industries such as the construction of dwellings (e.g. wattle for daubed walls), hurdle making (fences) for farming, and charcoal burning.

How to identify hazel...

- In the form of tall bushes and shrubs with clusters of 'rods' (straight poles of varying thicknesses).
- Rust coloured horizontal flecks on the rods.
- When freshly cut, or 'green', rods have enormous flexibility, nearly as much as willow, and great strength when woven.
- Most of the bushes seen today have been neglected. In the past they would have been cut to the base, or 'stool', every seven years so that the poles were of a uniform size. Usable green poles can be found, but they tend to be interspersed with unusable dead ones.

Tips on coppicing

Hazel thrives on being coppiced. It is best to coppice in the three months beginning in October when the leaves start to turn yellow. Cut as close to the ground as possible and always ask the landowner for permission first.

Woods with similar properties

Ash, willow, sycamore and sweet chestnut.

Willow

Willow grows best on wet ground. When looking for willow, head for wetlands, bogs, streams and rivers. Willow rods are extremely flexible and so very suitable for making baskets, hurdles, and all sorts of useful items. There are many different species of willow but the most common are Goat Willow (or Sallow) and Crack Willow. Willow can be easily grown by simply pushing a green stick into damp soil.

How to identify willow...

- Either found as trees or tall bushes and shrubs.

CRACK WILLOW

- Deciduous – loses its leaves in winter.
- Long, pointed, green leaves. Dull orange in autumn.
- Twig: dark brown in colour with rugged criss-crossing ridges.
- Catkins.

GOAT WILLOW

- Deciduous – loses its leaves in winter.
- Green, oval, wrinkly leaves, furry grey underside. Tip points slightly to one side.
- Twig: grey and quite thick. Reddish in the sun.
- Catkins.

Tips on coppicing

Harvesting willow is best done in the winter when all the leaves have fallen. Always ask the landowner for permission.

Birch

Birch is a suitable choice of wood for some of the projects outlined in this book.

Birch bark is a versatile material and can be used for a variety of purposes such as firelighting and making pouches and other containers. Never remove it from a live birch tree. Find a fallen or felled tree, better still sawn logs that often lie around woodlands. Find something that has been lying around for a while, but not for too long. If the bark has become inflexible and brittle, it has been left for too long. Use a knife to score through the bark first and then ease it off by undercutting with the knife as you pull it away. It can help to tap vigorously on the bark with a stick as you go.

How to identify birch...

- Bark: silvery white with dark, horizontal flecks.
- Small, heart-shaped leaves.

Cut bark away with knife

Elder

Some children describe the texture of elder bark as 'acne'. Perhaps an unpleasant association, but fairly accurate as a description! Elder was once a much prized tree because all parts of it, from the fruit and flower to the leaves and branches, had a practical use: from the flower, elderflower champagne, wine and cordial can be made; elderberry wine from the fruit; and its pungent leaves were once used to keep flies at bay. But it is the canes that provide a useful material for woodland crafts. The soft centre, or pith, can be easily pushed out using something flat-ended like a tent peg, leaving a wooden tube or bead, an invaluable resource, as I hope to demonstrate over the next few pages.

How to identify elder...

- Clusters of tiny white flowers and dark berries in spring and summer.
- Long curved 'canes' in winter, which once seen, can be easily spotted on the horizon.
- 'Acne' texture on bark.

Tips on coppicing

Coppicing is best done in winter when the plants are dormant.

Some useful knots and lashings

These knots and lashings will be very useful
for many of the ideas in this book.

Rather than trying to master them all at once,
try learning each as you need it for a
specific project. Having a genuine goal is
such an incentive!

Overhand knot

The overhand knot is very simple and useful.

Clove hitch

This knot forms the basis of a square lashing (page 20).

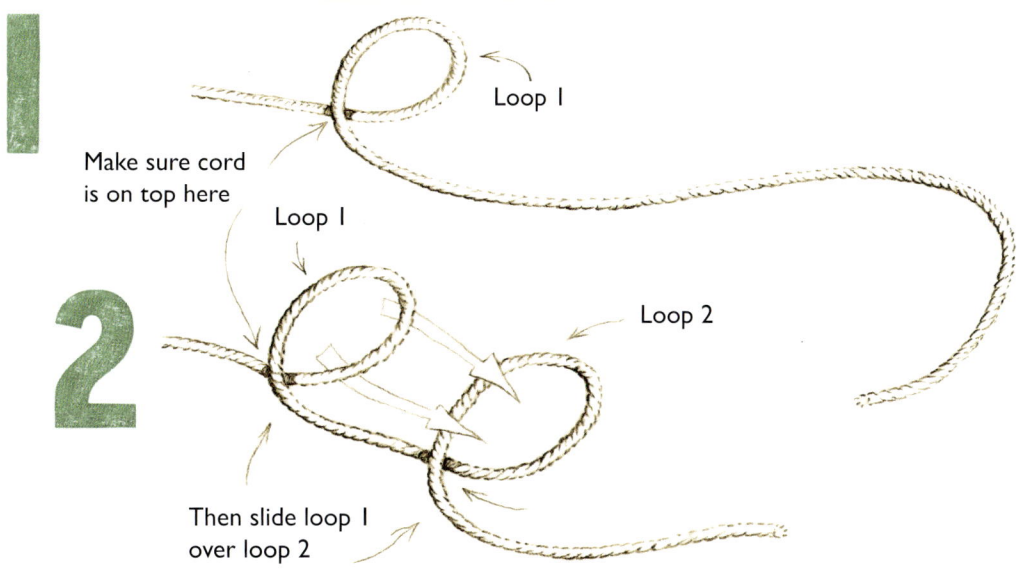

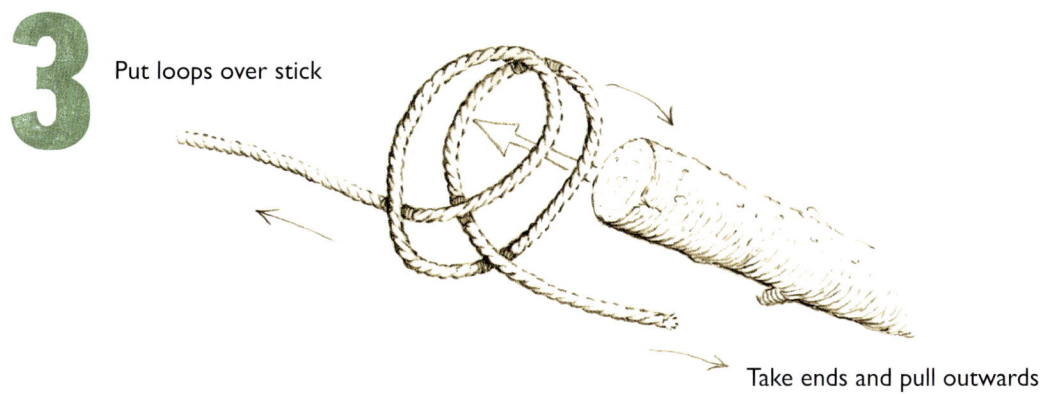

Square lashing

The square lashing is needed for many of the ideas in this book. It joins together poles that are placed square to one another.

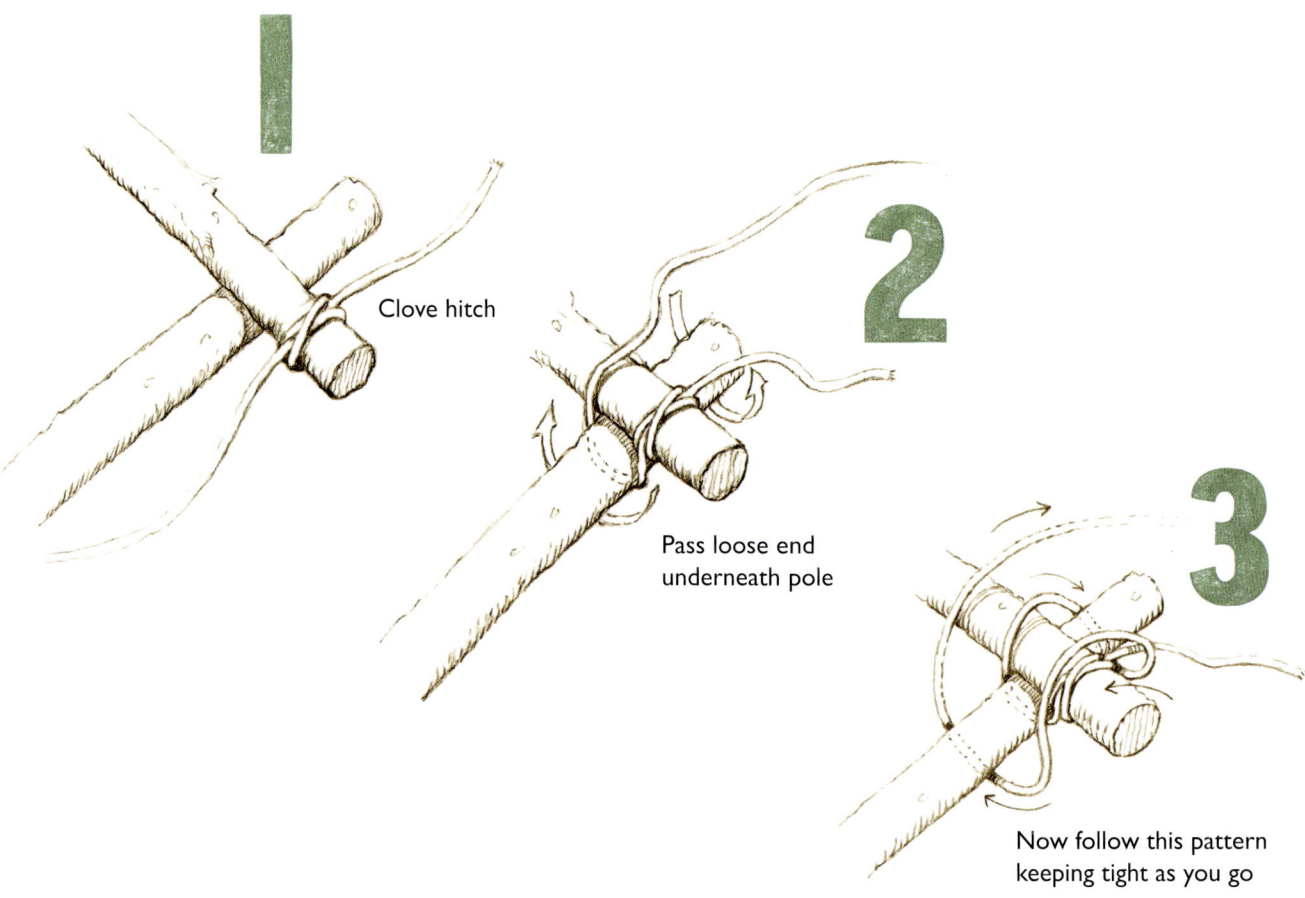

1. Clove hitch
2. Pass loose end underneath pole
3. Now follow this pattern keeping tight as you go

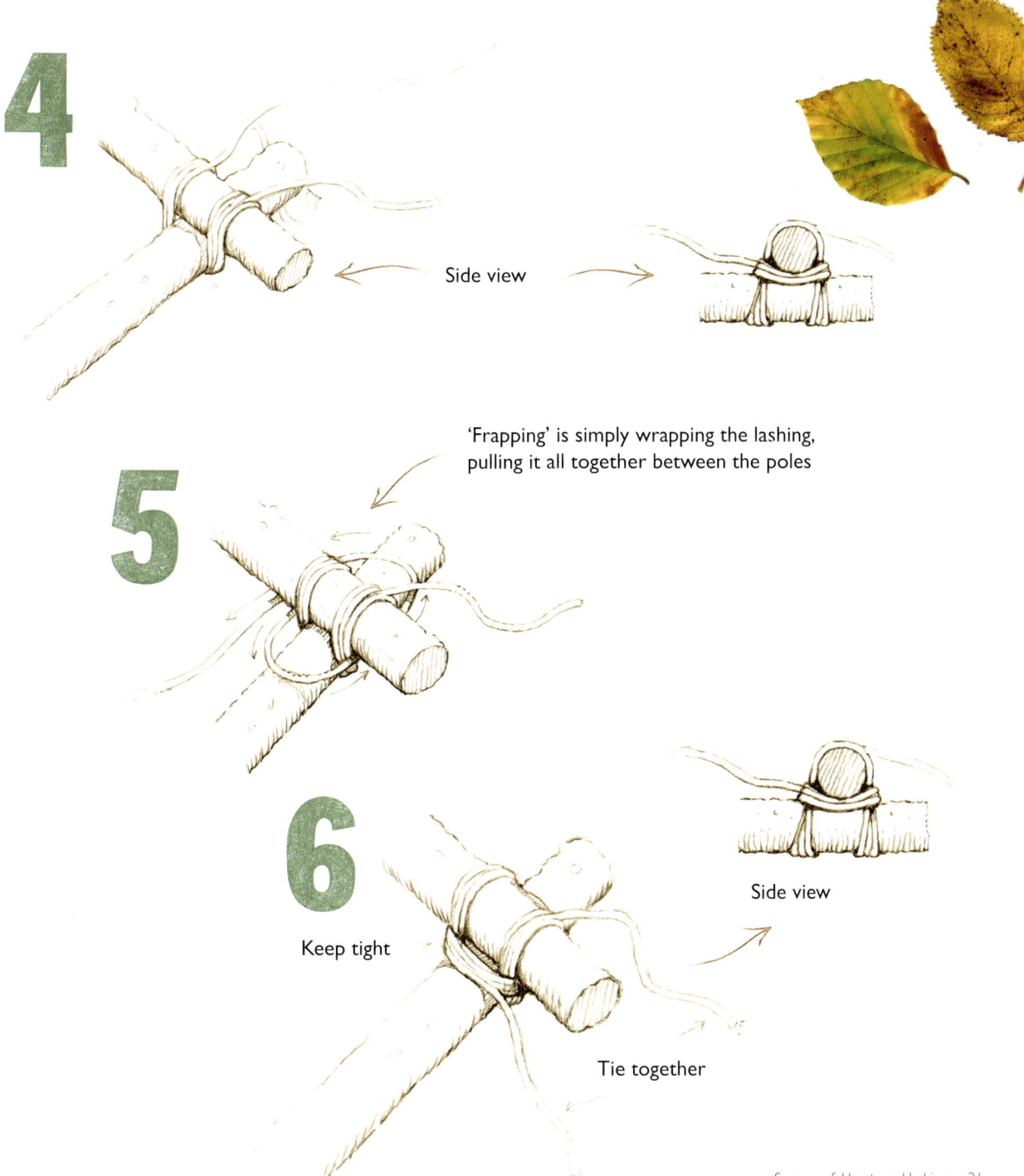

Side view

'Frapping' is simply wrapping the lashing, pulling it all together between the poles

Side view

Keep tight

Tie together

Some useful knots and lashings 21

Sheer lashing

The sheer lashing ties together poles which are placed alongside one another.

1 Clove hitch

2 Now wrap the loose end of the cord tightly around the two poles

3 Wrap the lashing and pull it together tightly between the poles

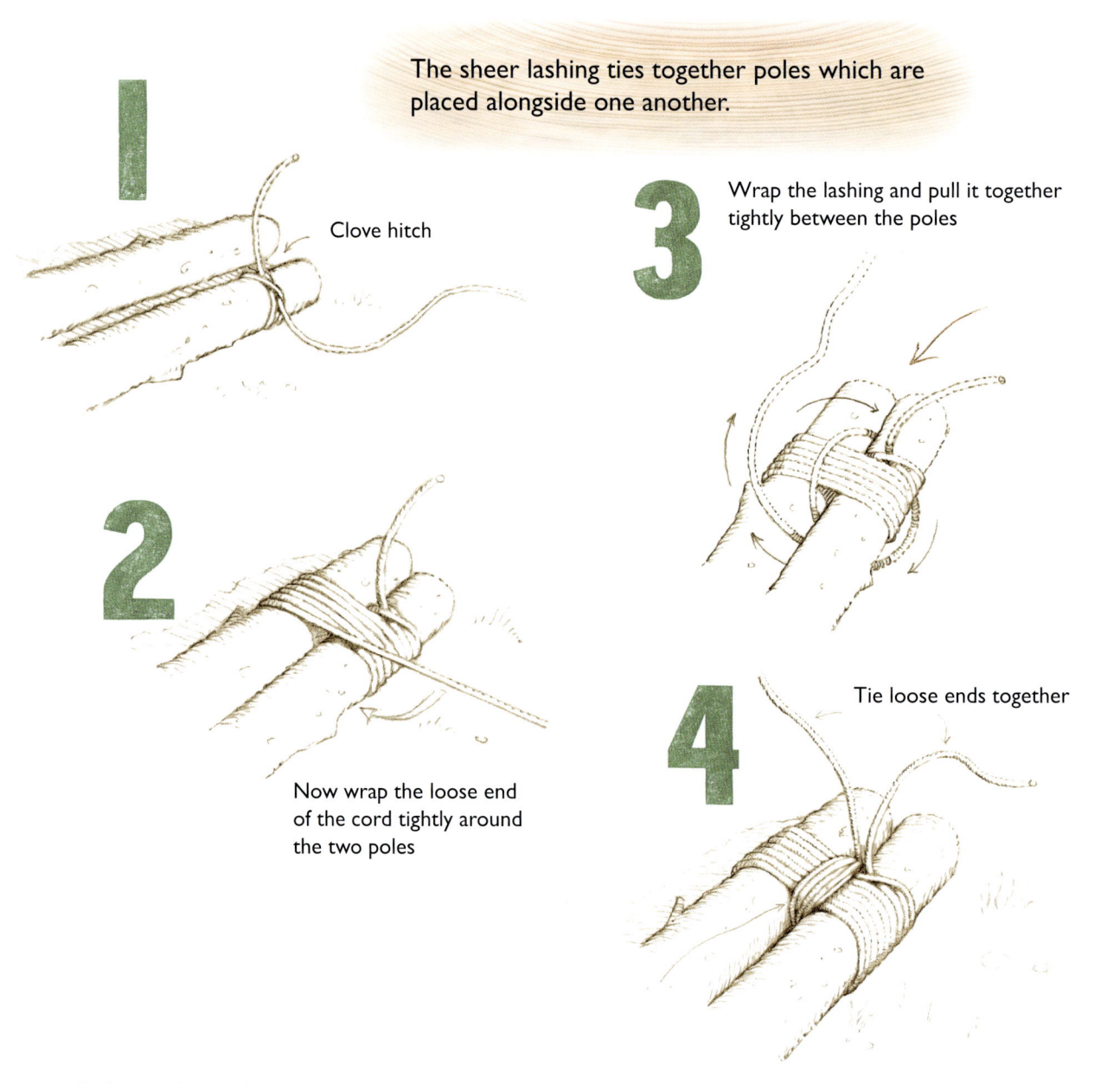

4 Tie loose ends together

Whipping

'Whipping' is the process of making a string grip for a handle. Make sure you have a very generous length of string.

Long enough at this end to get a good hand grip later

Make sure you use plenty of string

Continue wrapping cord around pole neatly

End through loop

Some useful knots and lashings 23

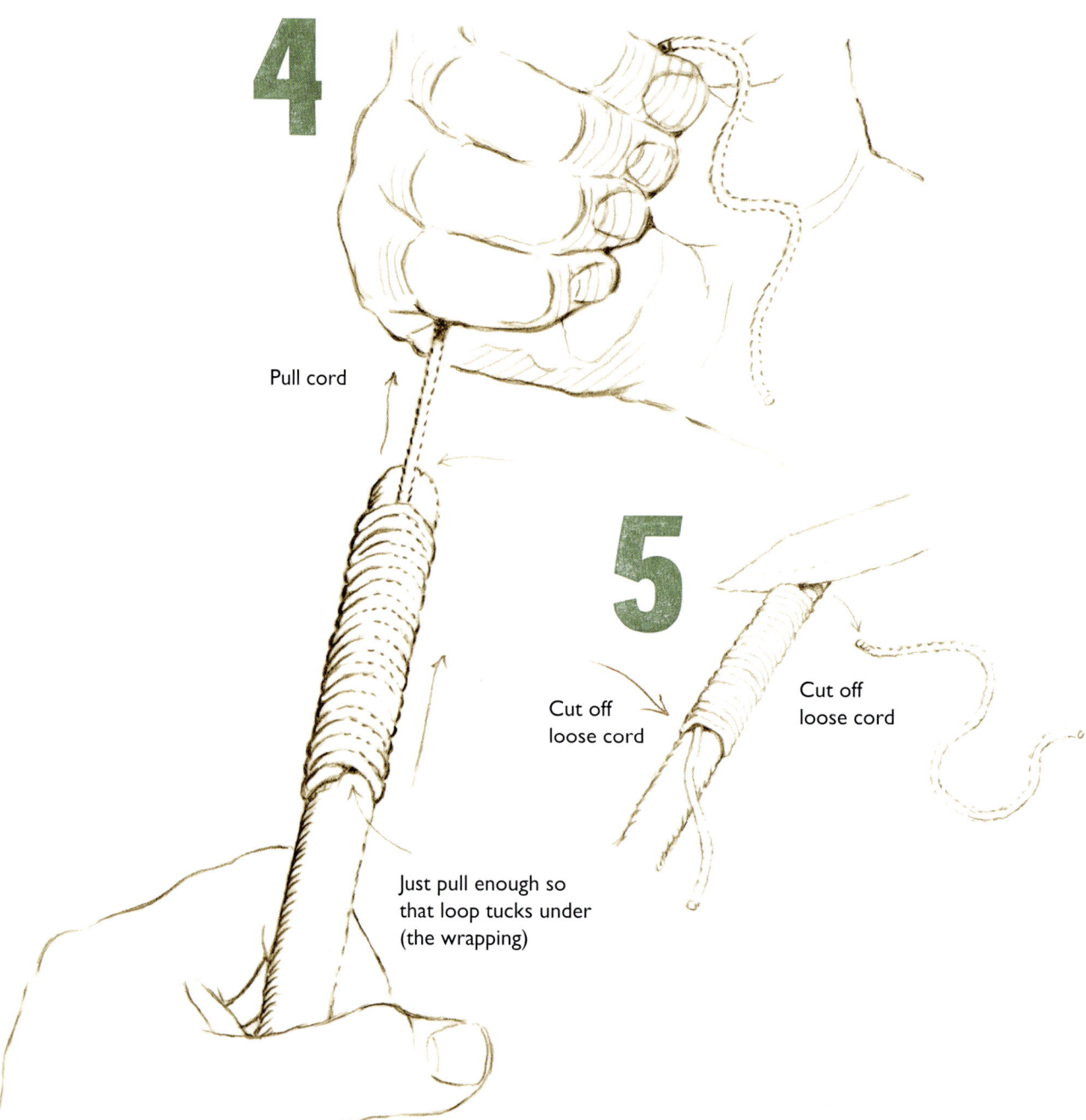

Netting

Netting can be used for doors, for shelters, for hammocks, bags, wigs, seats and much more.

This is called a 'Bite'

Prepare several long lengths of cord (depending on size of net). Half way along each length of cord form a 'bite' and attach to pole using a 'lark's foot' See page 26

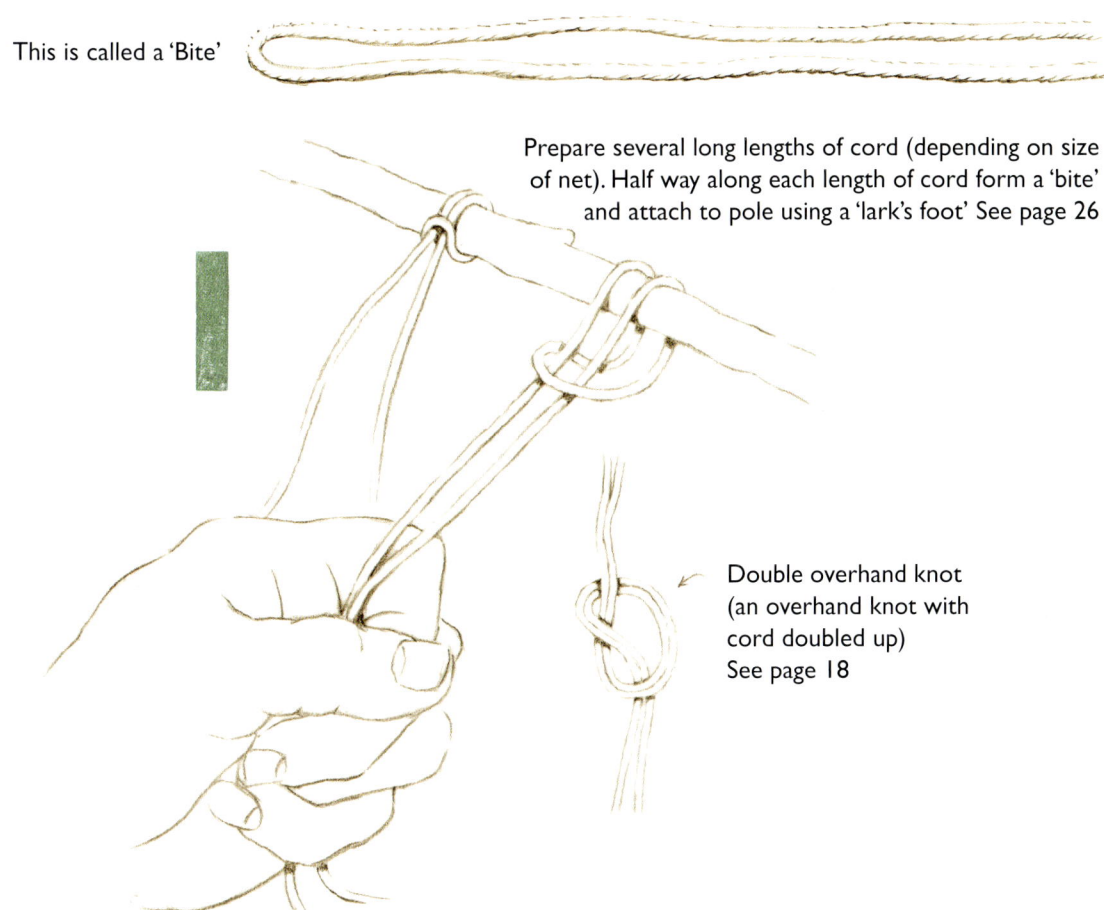

Double overhand knot (an overhand knot with cord doubled up) See page 18

Some useful knots and lashings

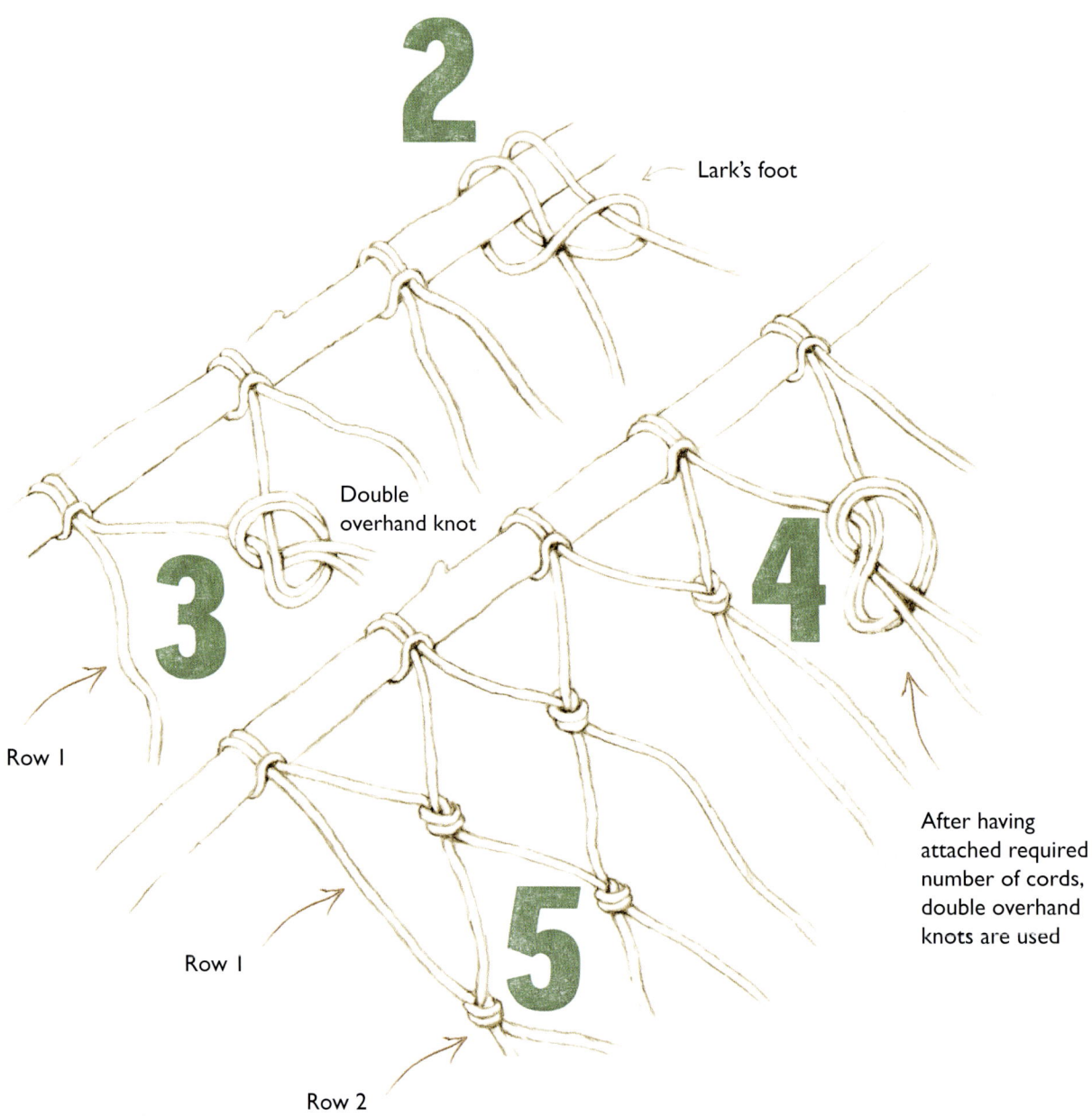

26 Some useful knots and lashings

Things to make

Freshly cut woods such as hazel and ash are fun to whittle because the grain 'gives way' more easily. Choosing a material that is easy to handle is an important factor when working with children or anyone with little experience or practice.

Hazel mask

Use tender, young shoots, and bend and wind into a loop like this

Masks are great for camouflage or woodland drama. You could make a stage and even a theatre out of natural materials.

Willow makes a more than adequate alternative to hazel.

These are the three basic shapes required to assemble your mask.

Use the same process to make a figure of eight shape too

And a smaller loop

2 Using twine, tie in the figure of eight shape and the hoop to make eyes and a mouth.
Add a straight rod to make the nose.
Make a grid with string or cotton by looping cotton or string around various points of the mask frame.

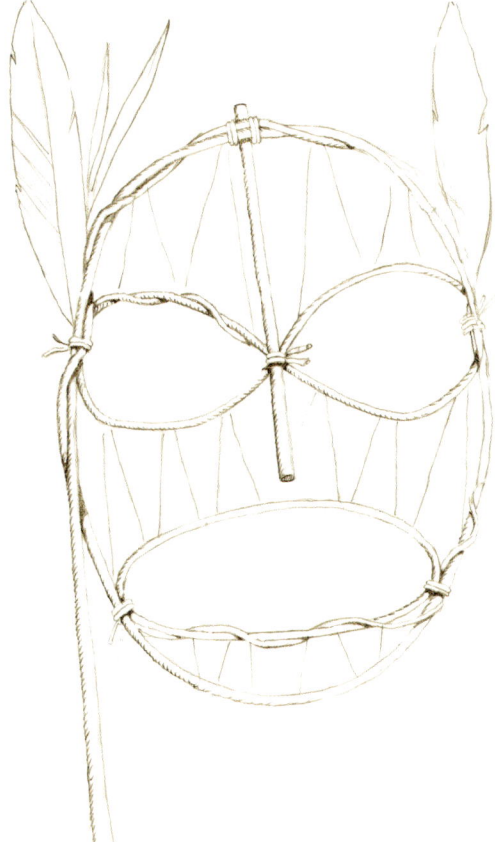

Tie with twine

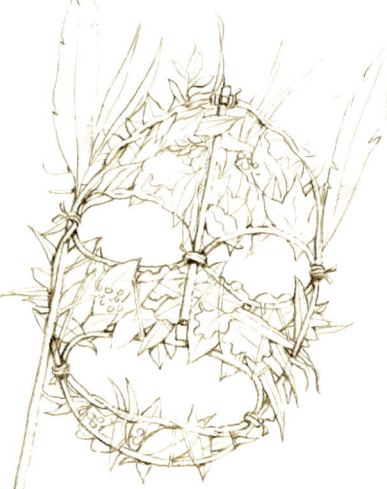

3 Leaves and moss can be pushed into various parts of the grid and mask frame

Things to make 29

Festive candle

1 Cut a length of fresh, green hazel and make a small hole in one end with a palm drill

Push a twig in too to hold the leaf upright

3 Find a leaf, which will become the 'flame' of your candle, and push it into the hole

2 Use a potato peeler or knife to make decorative markings in the bark of the hazel

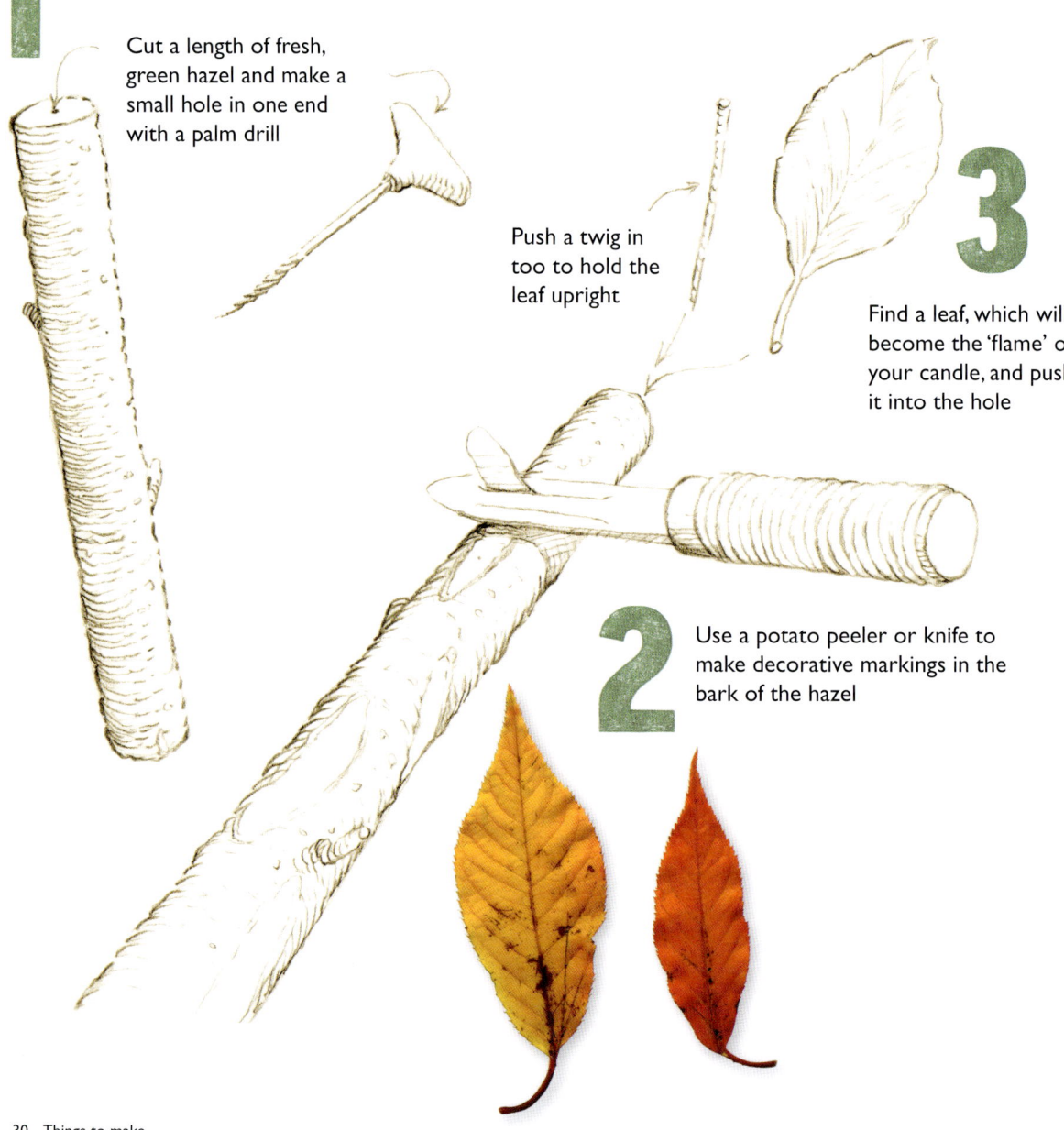

 Drill holes in a log and insert one or more of your 'festive candles' to make a candlestick holder

Mini hurdle

This project is a wonderful way to explore how weaving lengths of hazel can make strong structures.

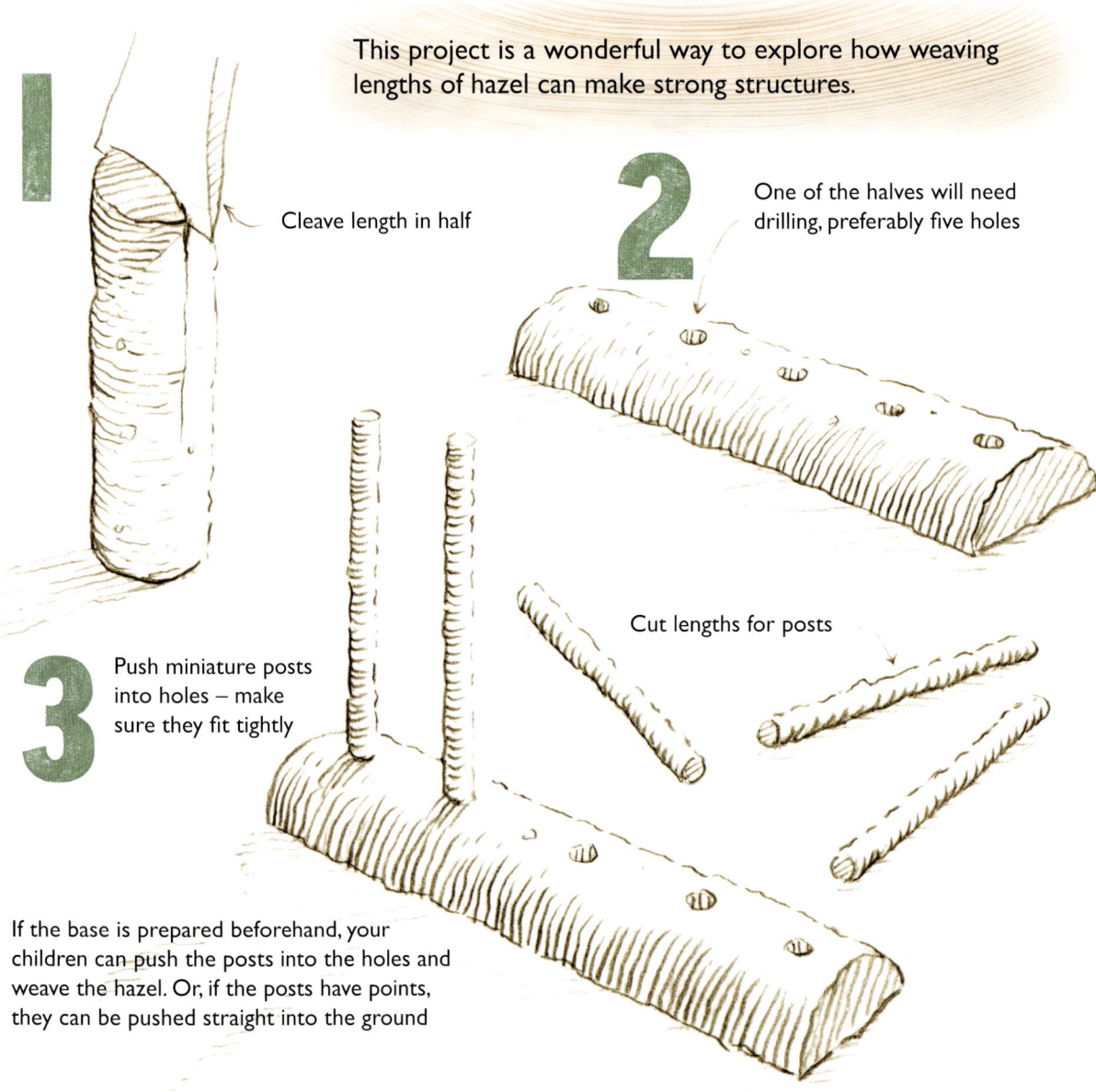

1. Cleave length in half
2. One of the halves will need drilling, preferably five holes
   Cut lengths for posts
3. Push miniature posts into holes – make sure they fit tightly

If the base is prepared beforehand, your children can push the posts into the holes and weave the hazel. Or, if the posts have points, they can be pushed straight into the ground

32　Things to make

4

Weave all the way to the top

Weave in hazel or willow, or other materials like grasses, twine or fabric

Things to make 33

French arrow

A French arrow does not need a bow. But feel free to use one.

1 Find some arrow-sized hazel rods. Make a cross in one end and split the rod part way down using a knife (enough to hold the 'feathers')

2 Find some birch bark

Make 'feathers' from your birch bark

Decide how big you want your 'feathers' to be, cut the bark into oblongs accordingly and fold in half

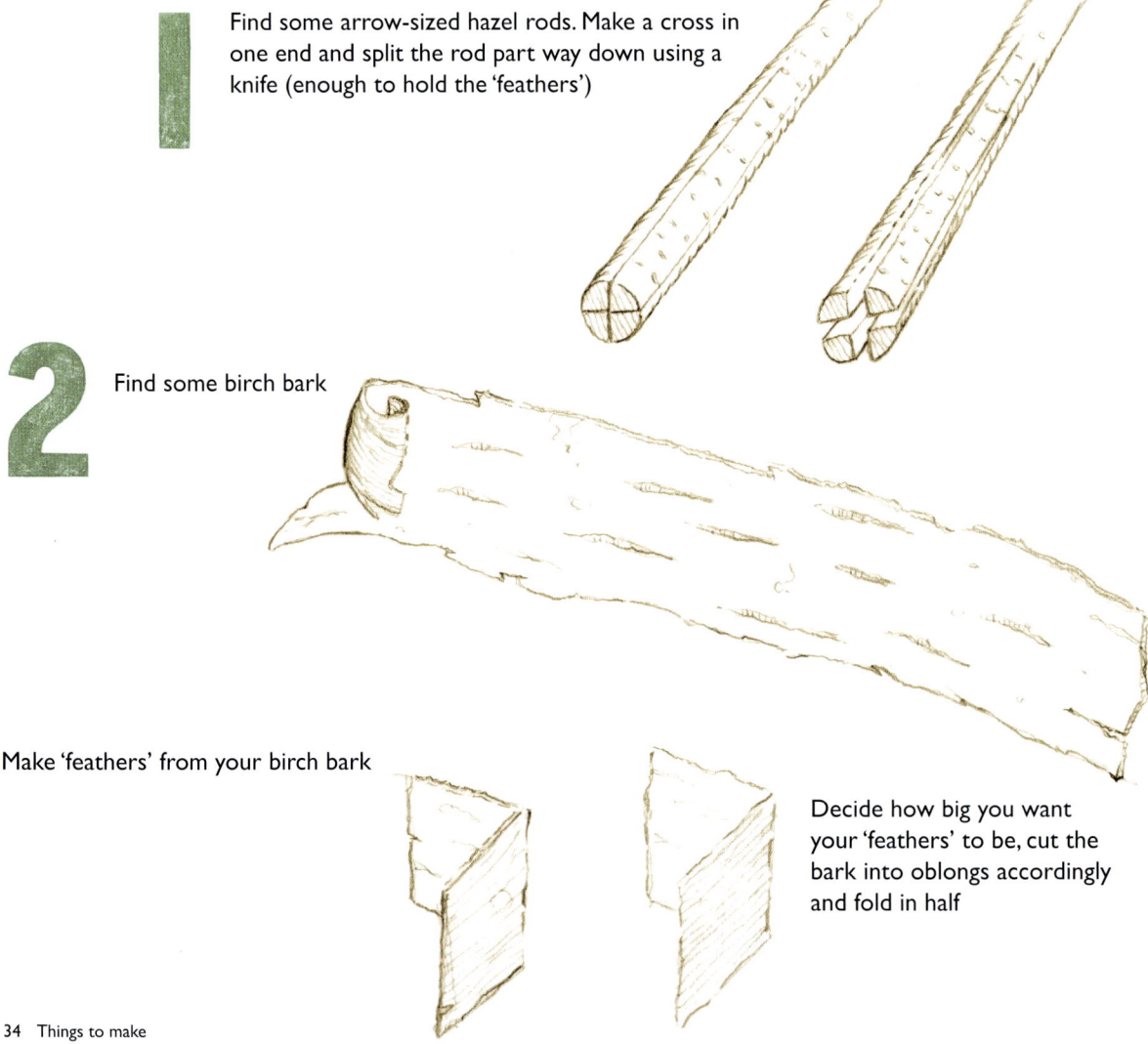

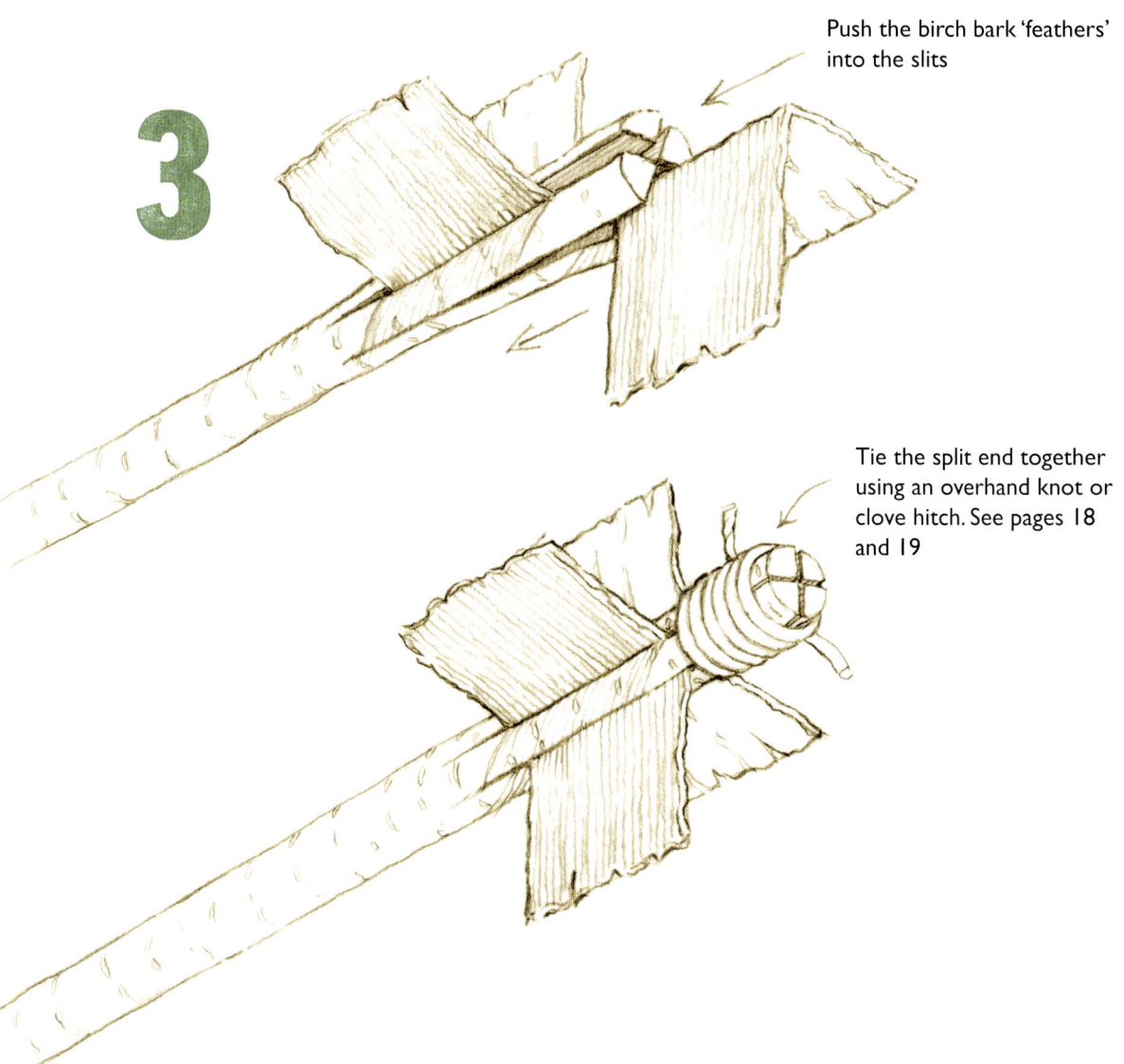

3

Push the birch bark 'feathers' into the slits

Tie the split end together using an overhand knot or clove hitch. See pages 18 and 19

Whittle a point for your arrow

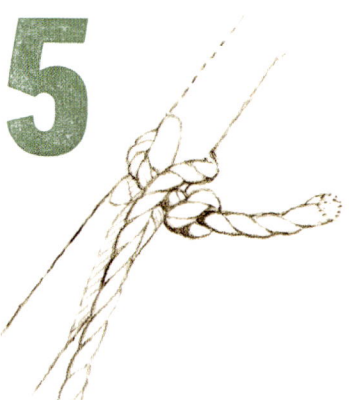

Make a notch in the shaft, then tie a knot in the end of the length of string and attach as shown

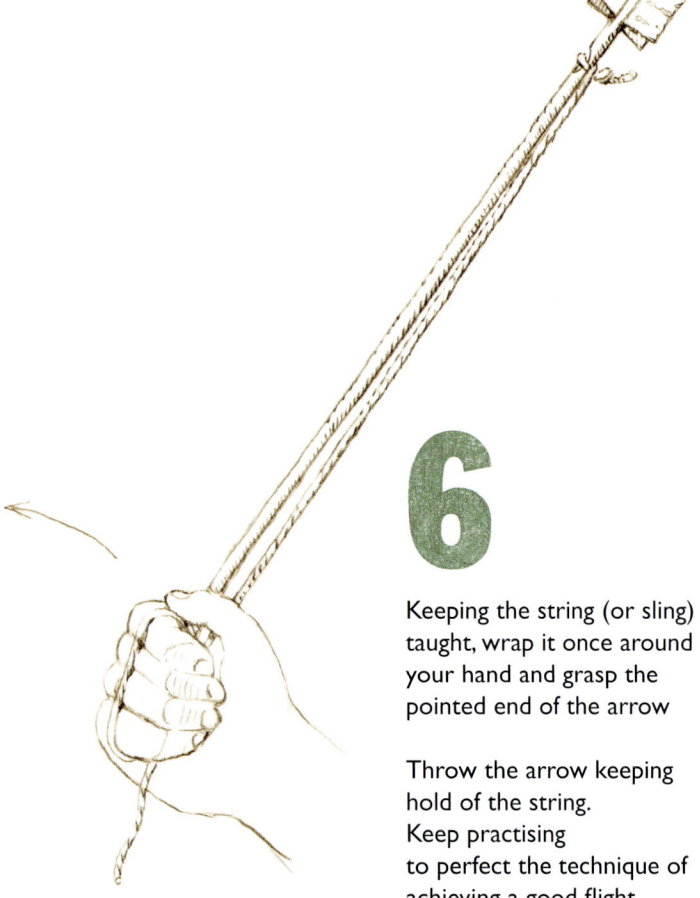

Keeping the string (or sling) taught, wrap it once around your hand and grasp the pointed end of the arrow

Throw the arrow keeping hold of the string.
Keep practising
to perfect the technique of achieving a good flight

Night torch

These torches, staked beside a fire at night, create a rich spectacle of light.

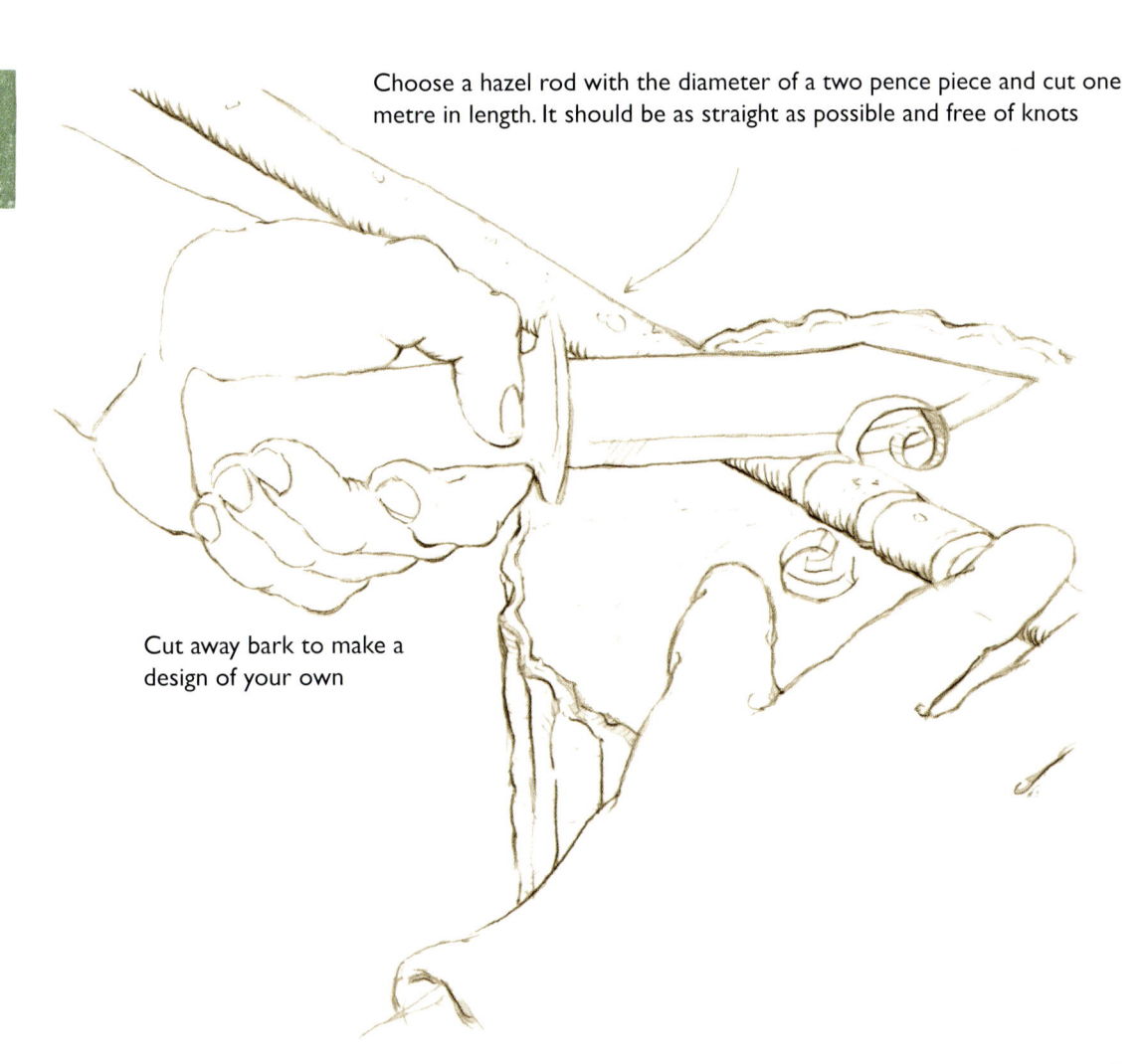

Choose a hazel rod with the diameter of a two pence piece and cut one metre in length. It should be as straight as possible and free of knots

Cut away bark to make a design of your own

Things to make 37

2
Cut a small split in this end

3
Find some birch bark

Fold it like this

And push it into the slit

4
Insert a night light or candle depending on size of loop

Make a point at this end and push the torch into the ground

38 Things to make

Dead hedging

Dead hedges are a useful way of making fencing, walls or wind breaks from dead wood. They also provide a good habitat for wildlife.

1 Make points at ends of four posts and drive into the ground

2 Dead wood is placed between the posts

Things to make 39

Staff

Every adventure requires a staff, and choosing the right stick to walk a hundred miles takes time and patience. Finding the right stick though, is an all-important task, and decorating the staff can be an ongoing project as you come across new found objects along the way.

Whittle your staff to make a design of your own

When whittling always work with the knife pointing away from your body

Whittle a point at the bottom end so it can be driven into the ground (then you can use both hands to decorate it)

Whittle a comfortable place for your thumb to rest if you like

40   Things to make

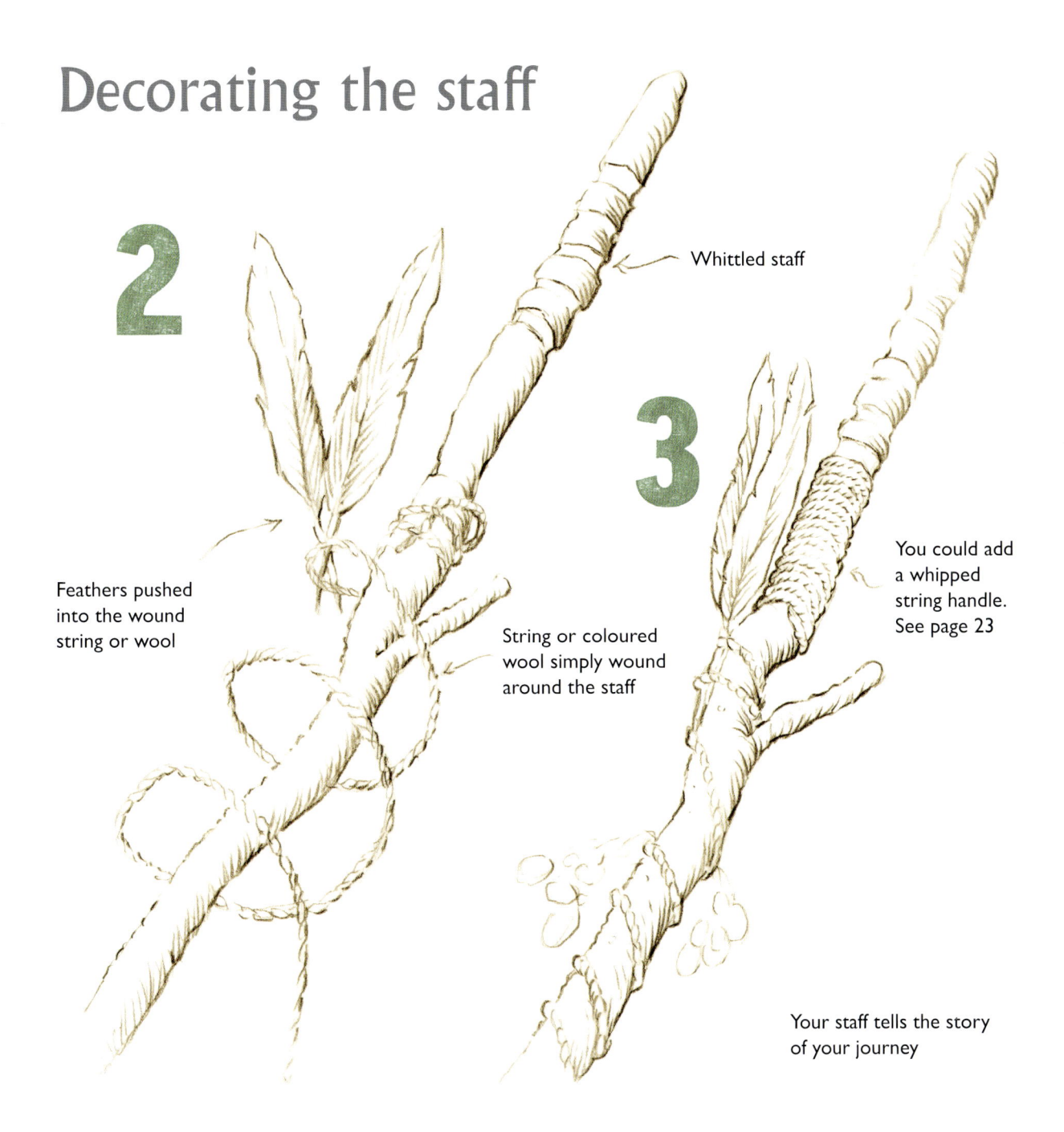

Decorating the staff

2

Whittled staff

Feathers pushed into the wound string or wool

String or coloured wool simply wound around the staff

3

You could add a whipped string handle. See page 23

Your staff tells the story of your journey

Things to make 41

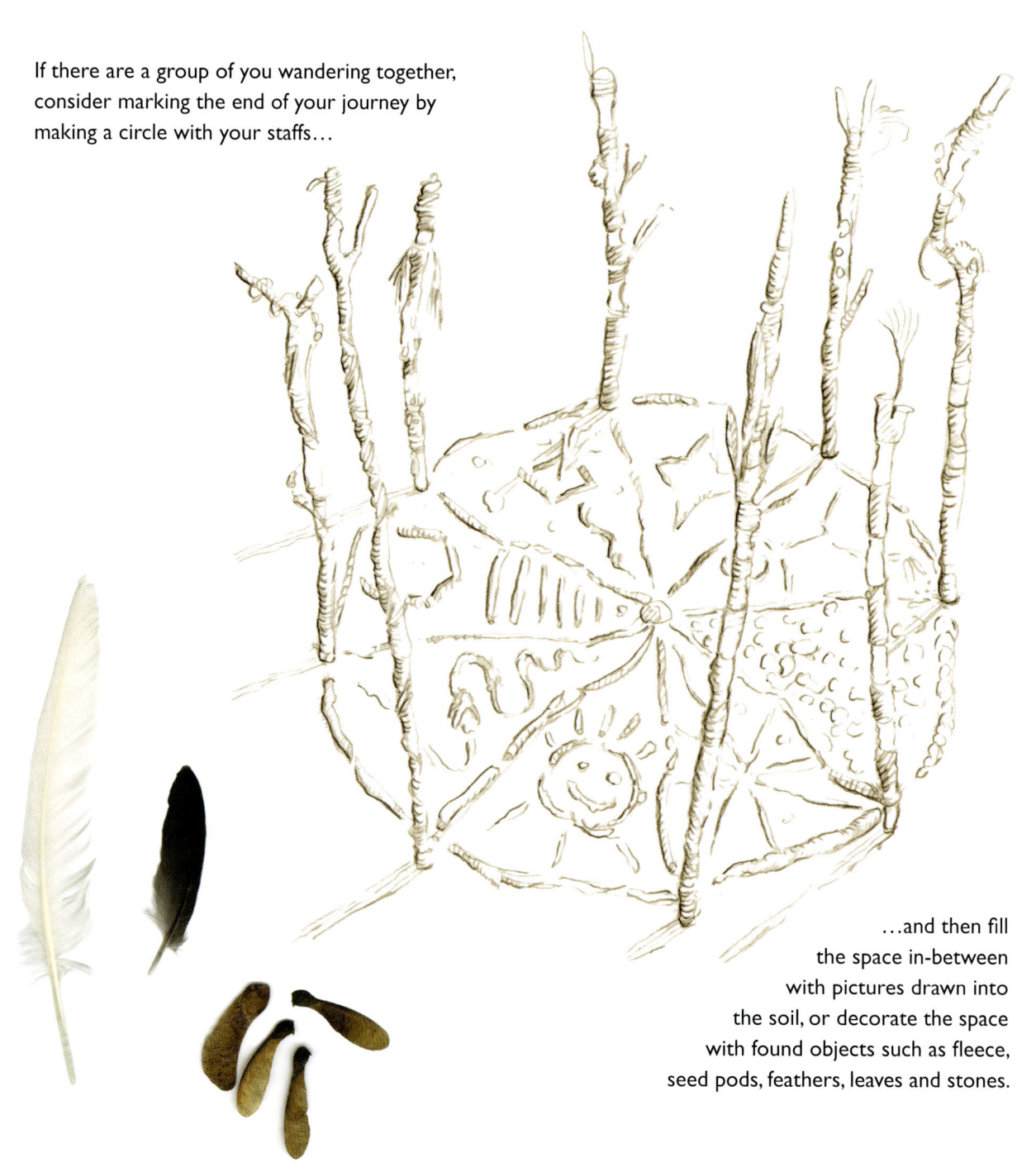

If there are a group of you wandering together, consider marking the end of your journey by making a circle with your staffs…

…and then fill
the space in-between
with pictures drawn into
the soil, or decorate the space
with found objects such as fleece,
seed pods, feathers, leaves and stones.

42 Things to make

Making and mending tools

Whipping, as described on page 23, can be useful for making and mending handles for tools, when you need to join two halves of a hazel rod together.

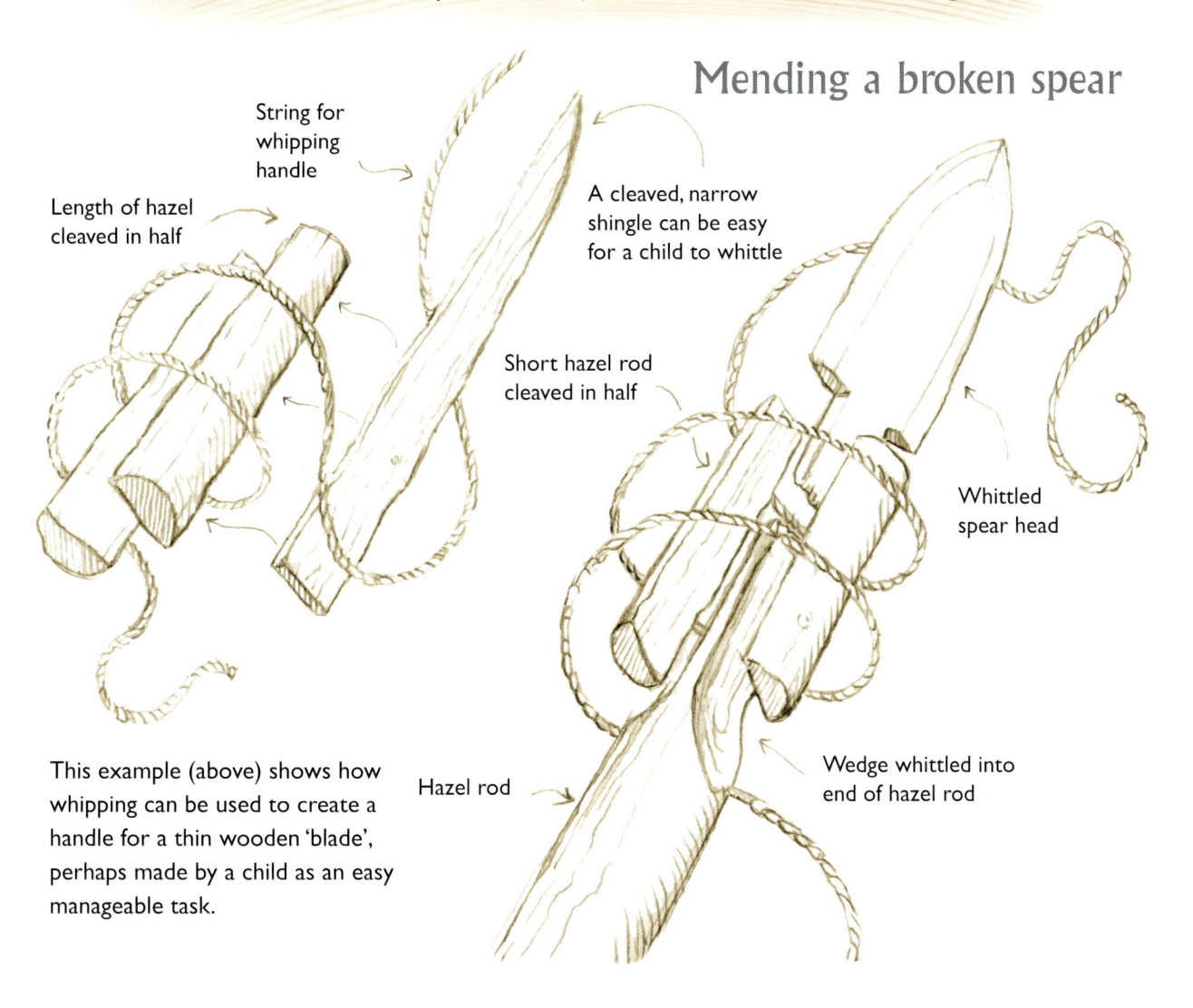

Mending a broken spear

String for whipping handle

Length of hazel cleaved in half

A cleaved, narrow shingle can be easy for a child to whittle

Short hazel rod cleaved in half

Whittled spear head

Hazel rod

Wedge whittled into end of hazel rod

This example (above) shows how whipping can be used to create a handle for a thin wooden 'blade', perhaps made by a child as an easy manageable task.

Things to make 43

Knife

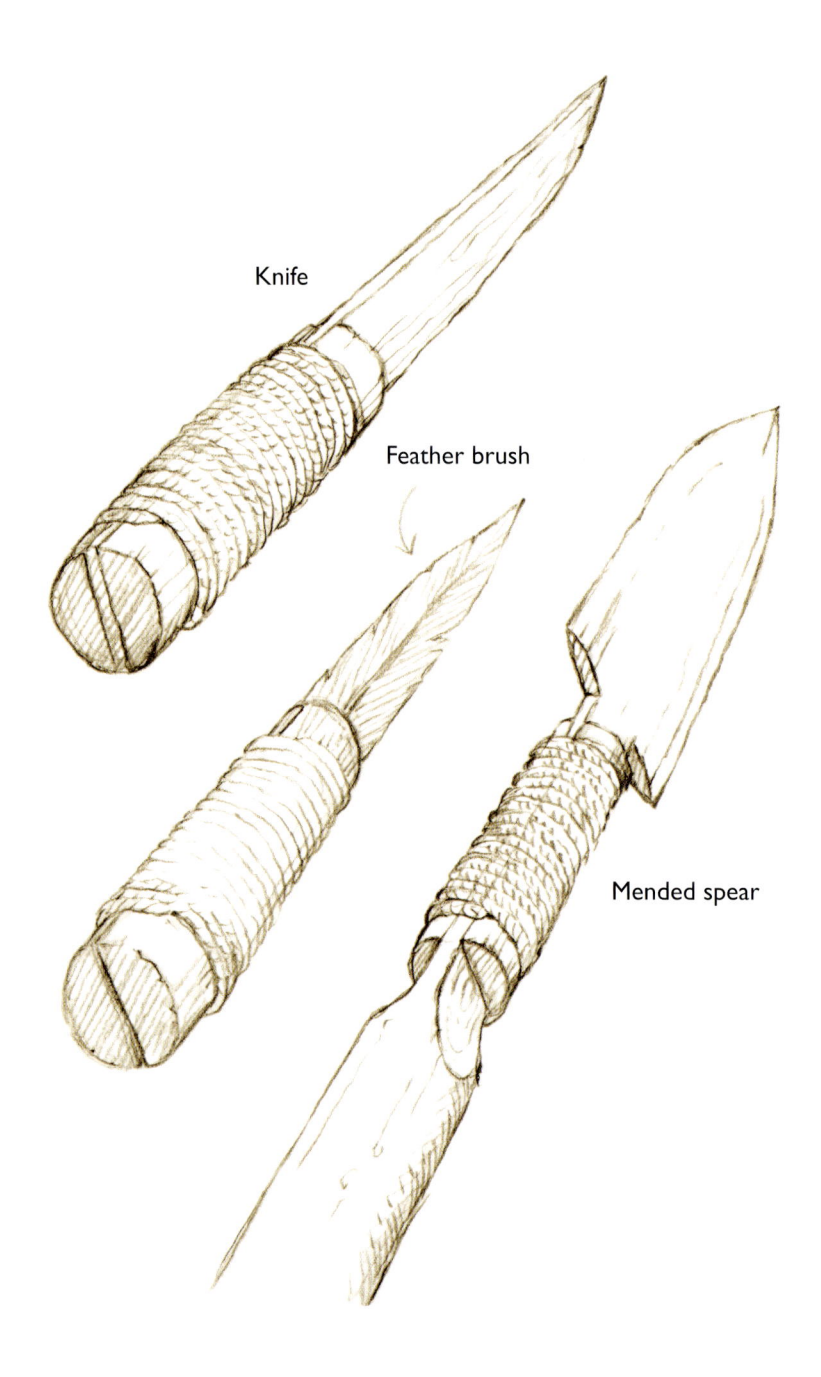

Feather brush

Mended spear

Making frames and simple structures

By effectively connecting poles at right angles, the square lashing is ideal for making frames and structures.

I hope that the following examples will inspire you to explore further.

Nature picture

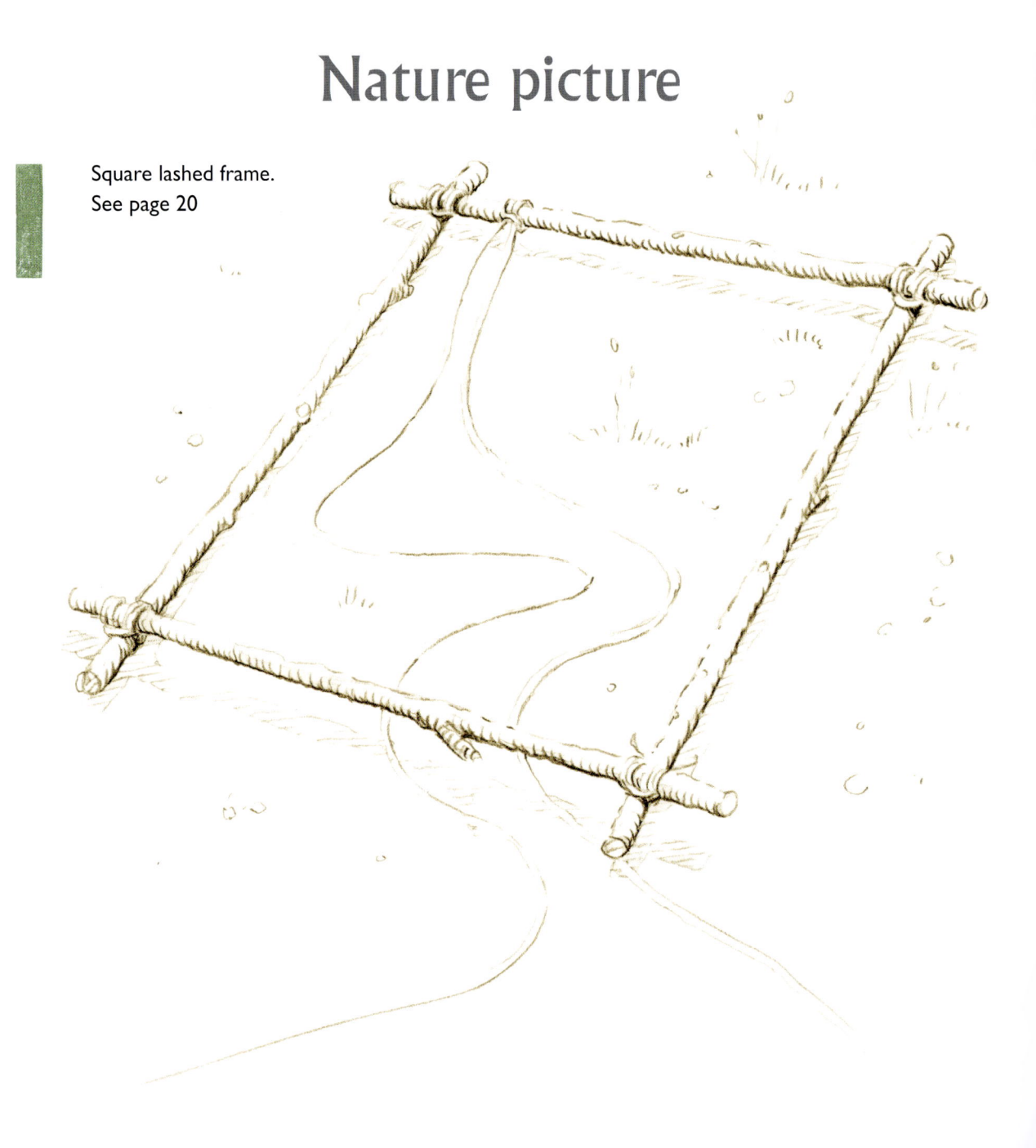

Square lashed frame.
See page 20

2 Add netting (see page 25)...

- Feathers
- Grasses
- Netting
- Leaves
- Moss

...and make a picture with natural materials

Making frames and simple structures 47

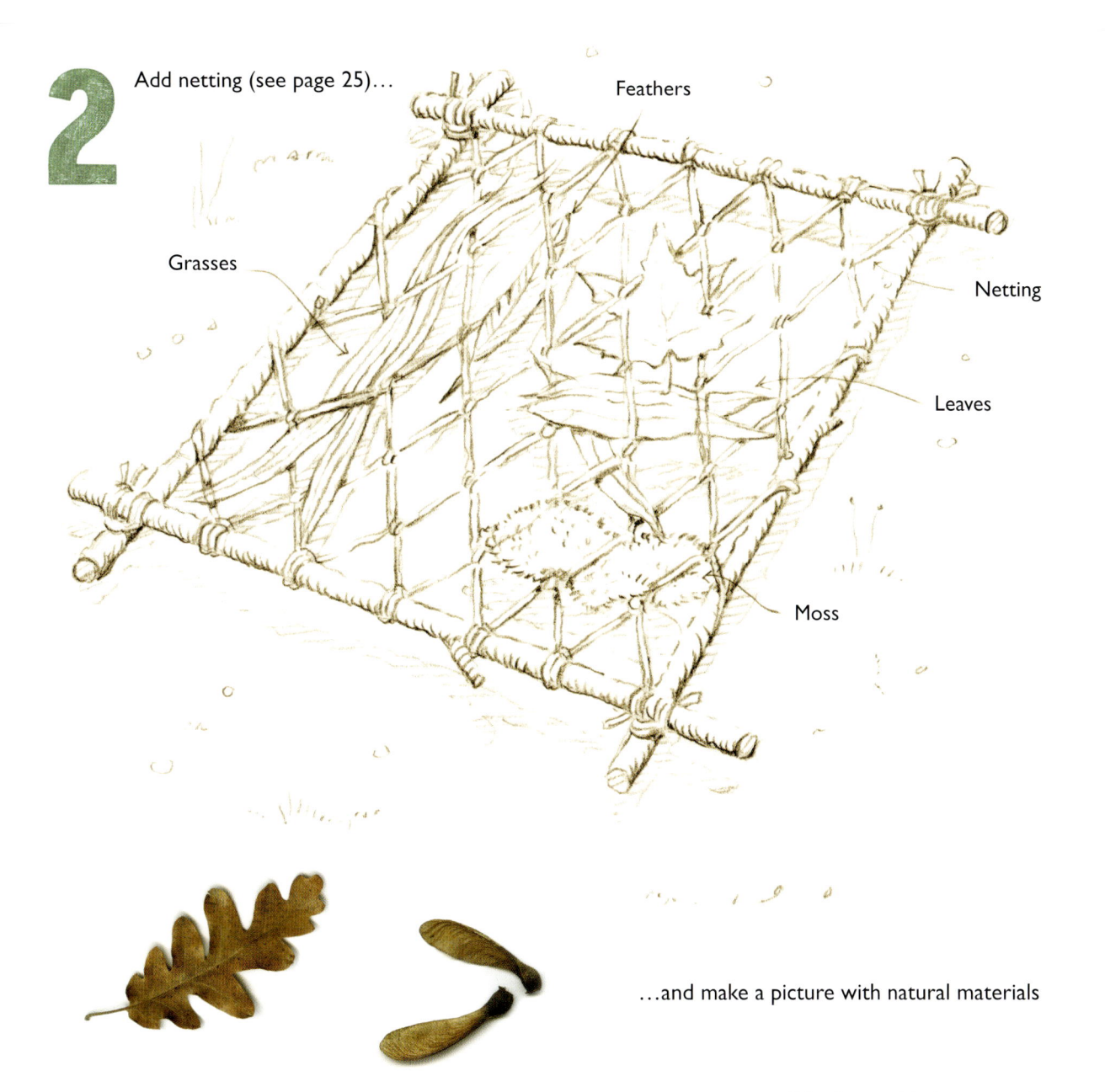

Ladder

Ladders can take you to new worlds only found up in the tree tops.

They are also useful when working in the woods, for example when putting up tarpaulins to make a shelter.

Stretcher

Fun to use in play, stretchers can also have an important function in the woods. Imagine someone hurts themselves and you need to carry them out quickly! These can quite easily be adapted to make bridges.

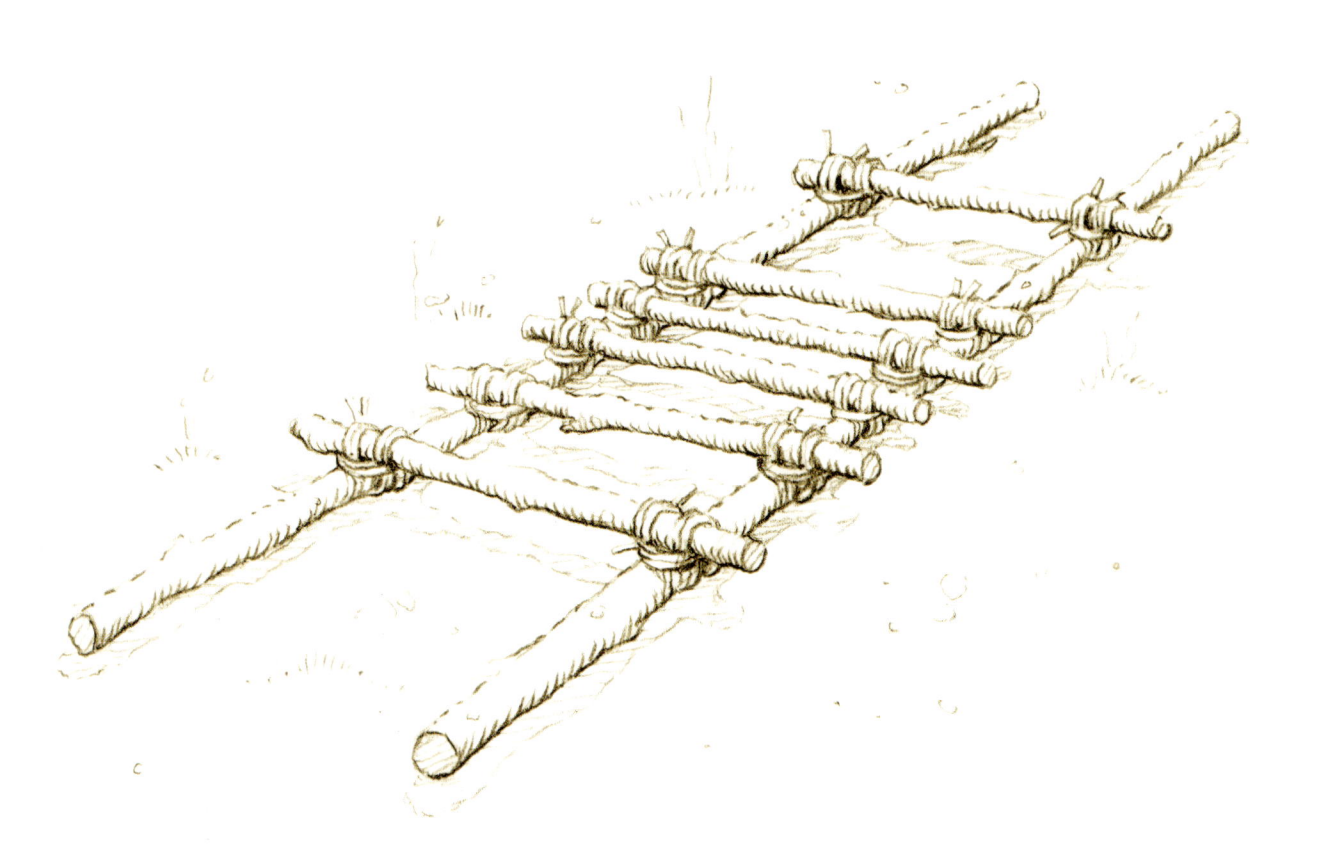

Star gazer

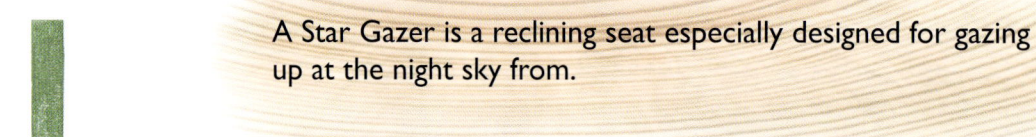

A Star Gazer is a reclining seat especially designed for gazing up at the night sky from.

Find four straight, strong poles about your own height and lay them in pairs on the ground. Sheer lash them at one end. See page 22

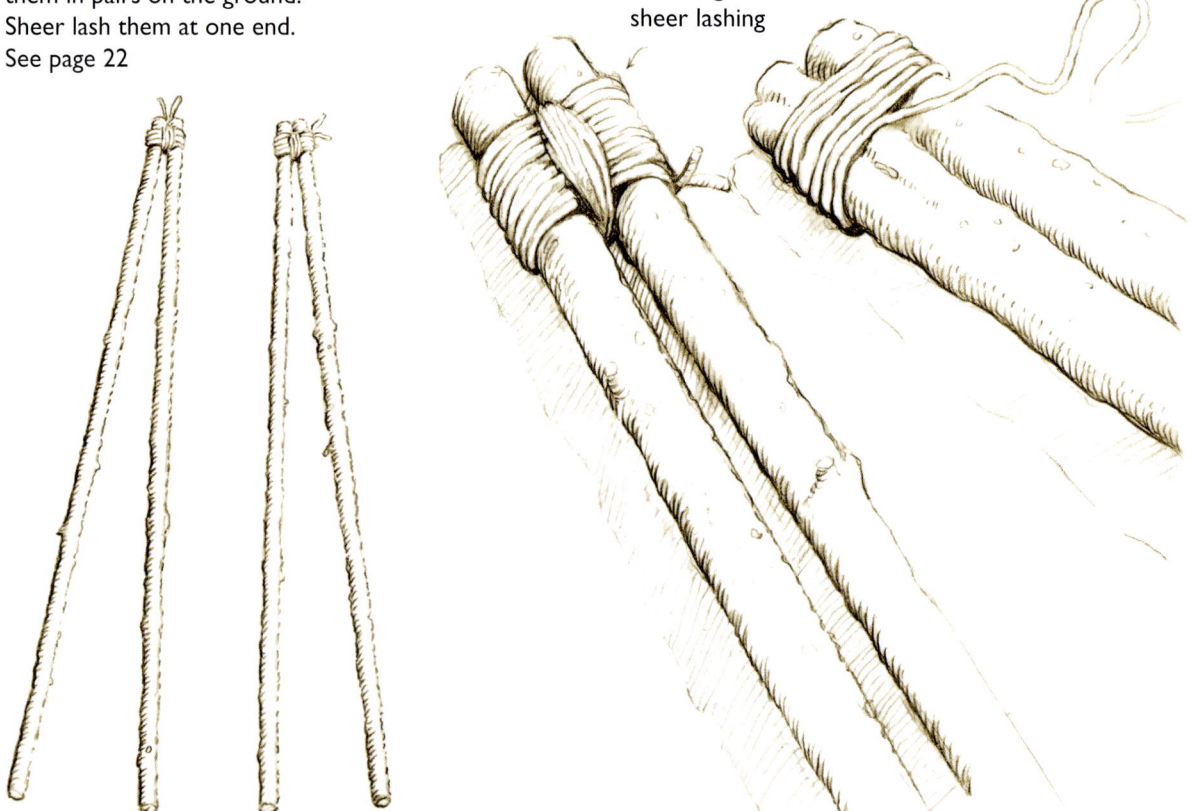

Good tight sheer lashing

50　Making frames and simple structures

2

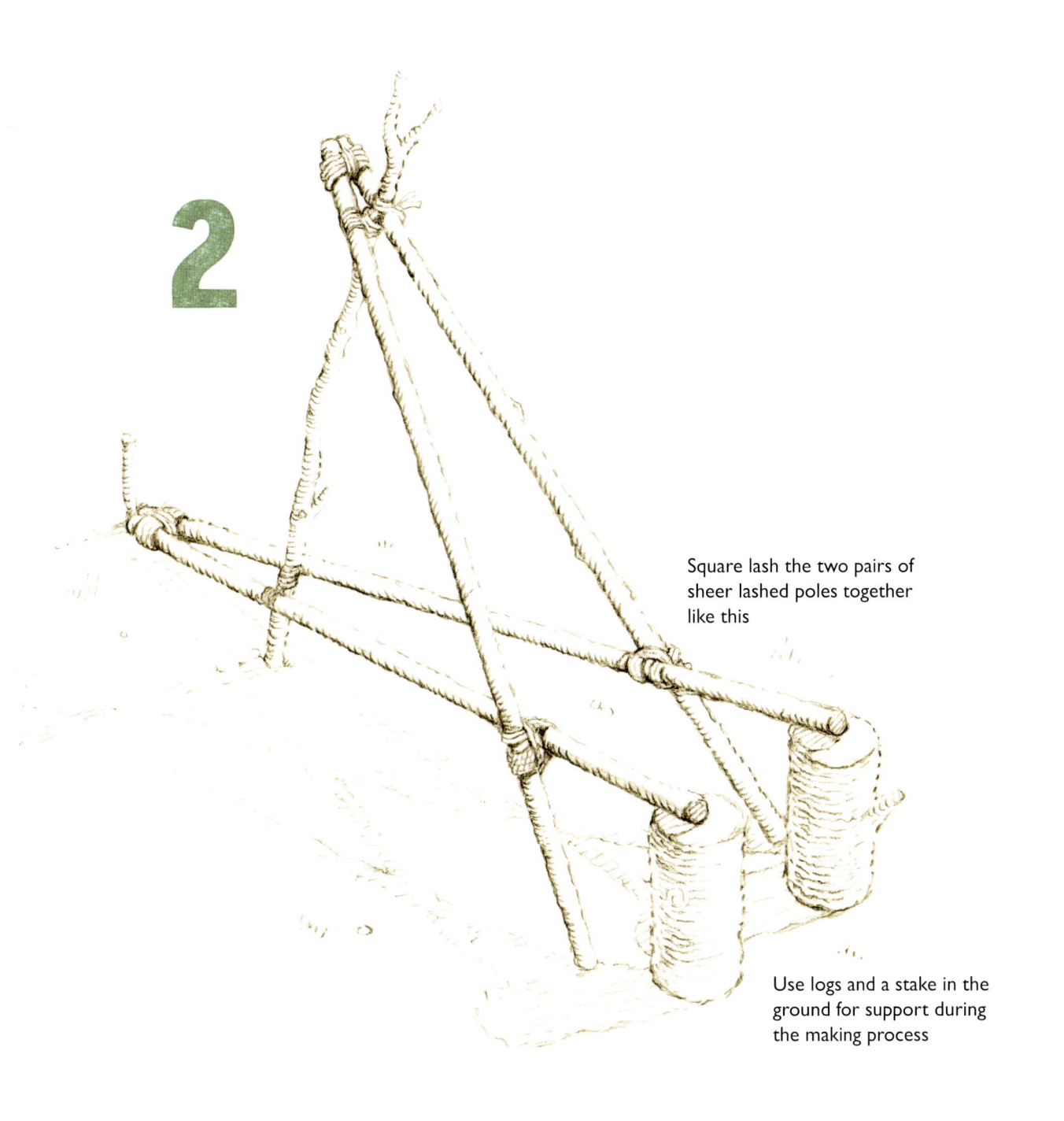

Square lash the two pairs of sheer lashed poles together like this

Use logs and a stake in the ground for support during the making process

Making frames and simple structures 51

3

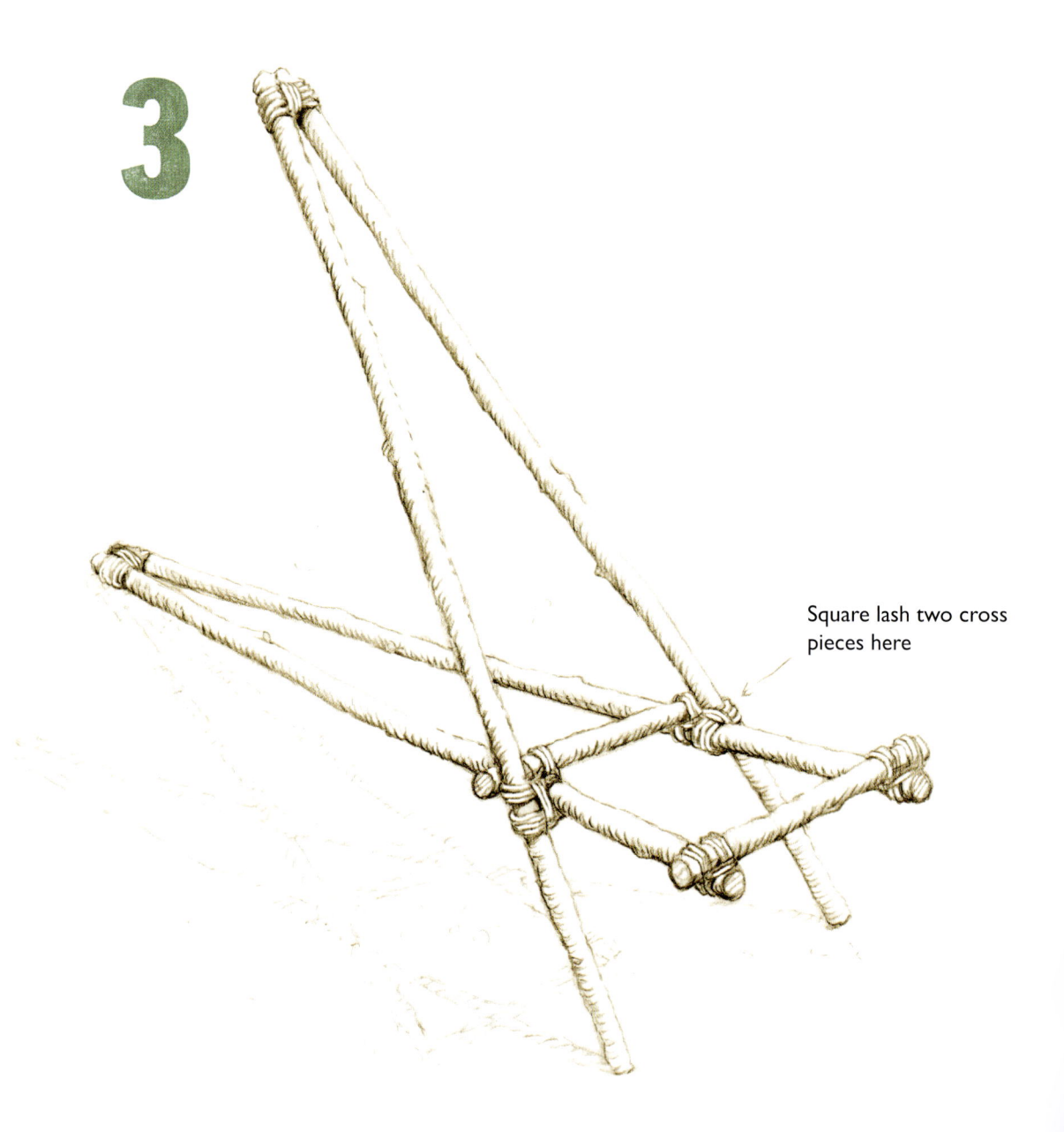

Square lash two cross pieces here

4

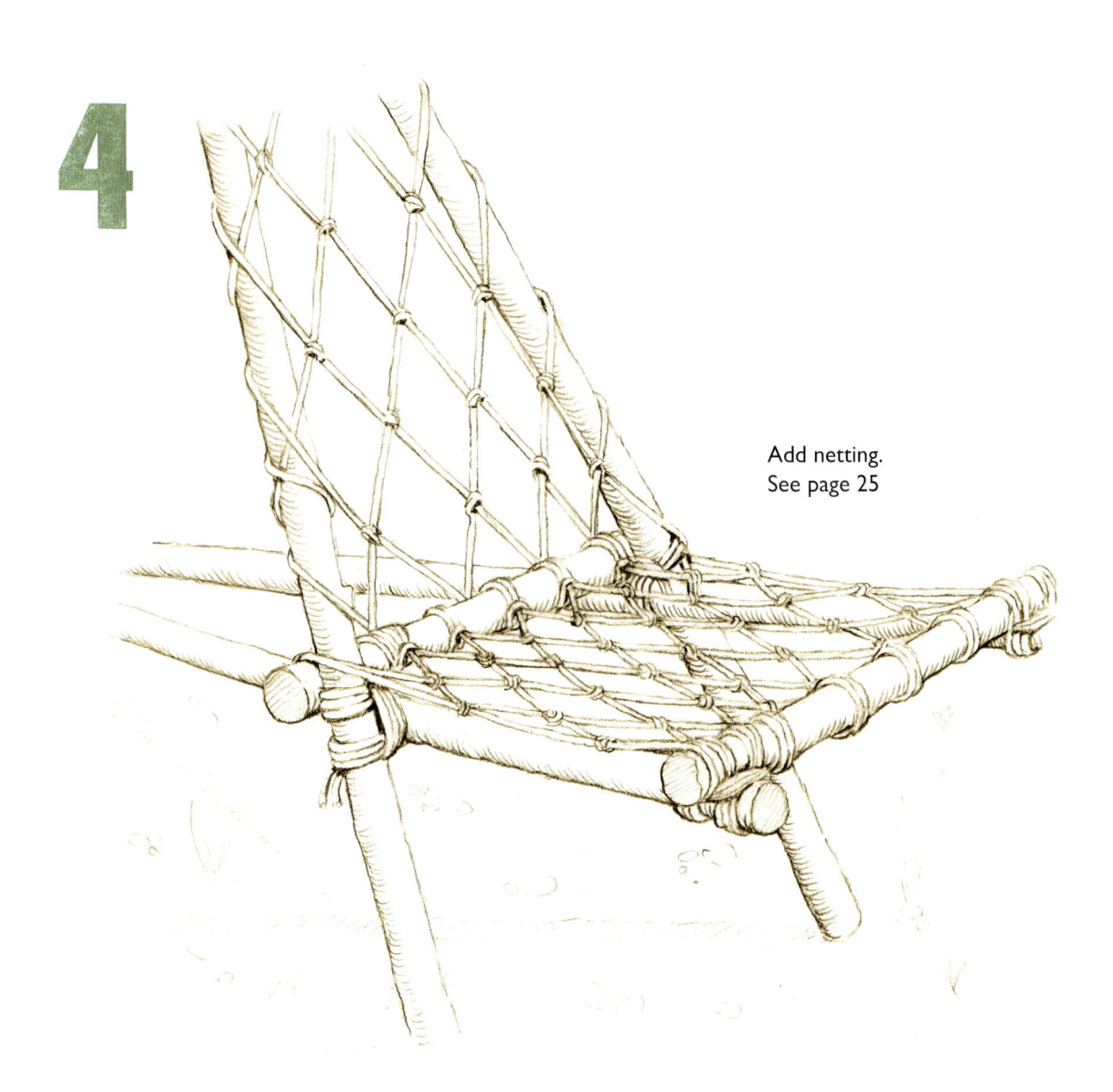

Add netting.
See page 25

Making frames and simple structures 53

The tripod

The tripod is a simple device with plenty of useful applications. And it is easy to make.

Making a tripod

A cloth or tarpaulin thrown over a tripod creates a good den.

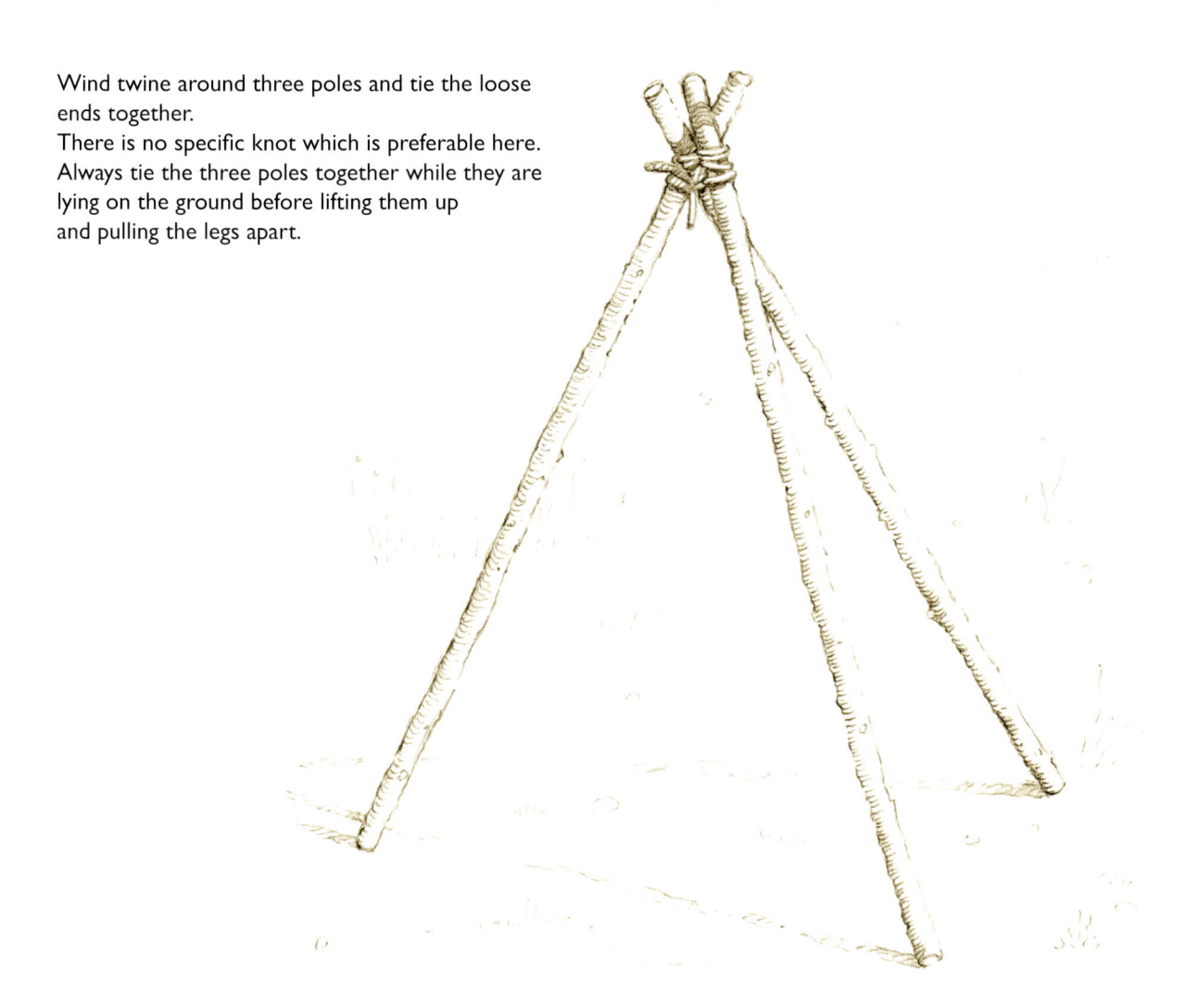

Wind twine around three poles and tie the loose ends together.
There is no specific knot which is preferable here. Always tie the three poles together while they are lying on the ground before lifting them up and pulling the legs apart.

You can make large shelters or tunnels by linking individual tripods together using ridge poles placed between them

Construct a simple tipi shelter by making a tripod first, and then add more poles and dead wood, securing them at the top

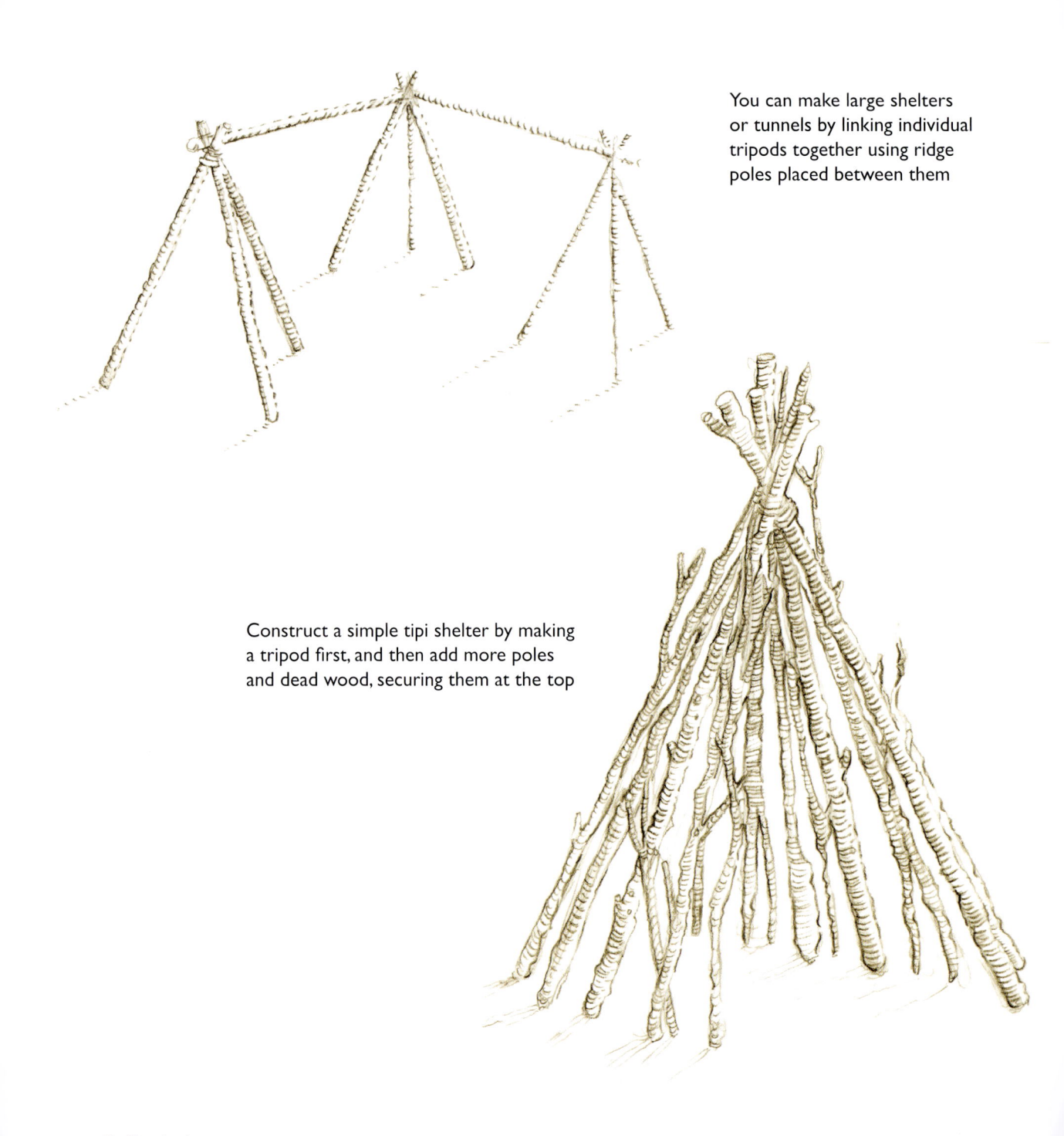

Tripod seat

Transform a tripod into a seat by attaching four poles of wood using the square lashing.

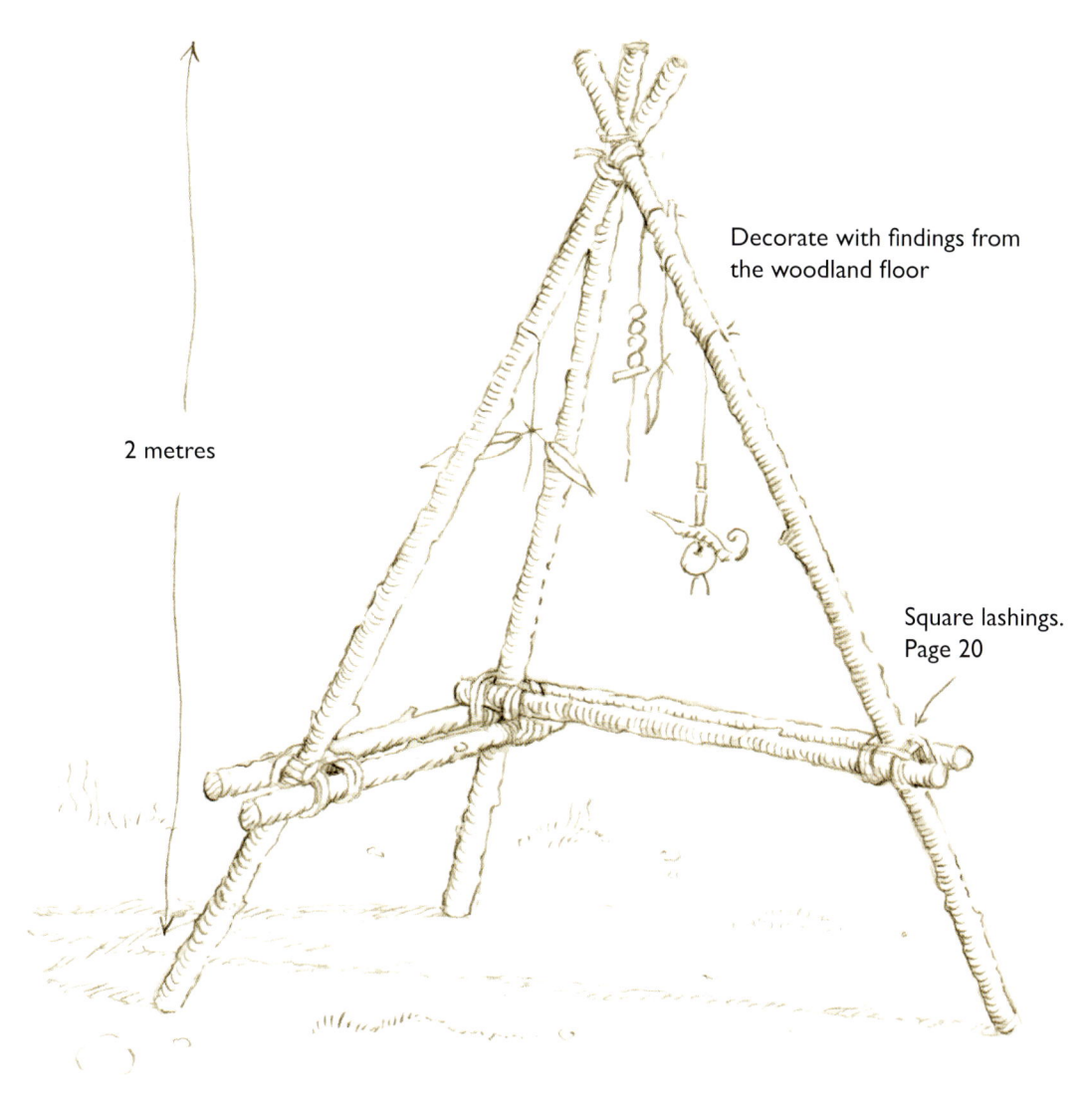

Decorate with findings from the woodland floor

2 metres

Square lashings.
Page 20

The tripod 57

Tripod monsters

Use tripods to create crazy animals and monsters which are strong enough to climb on and ride!

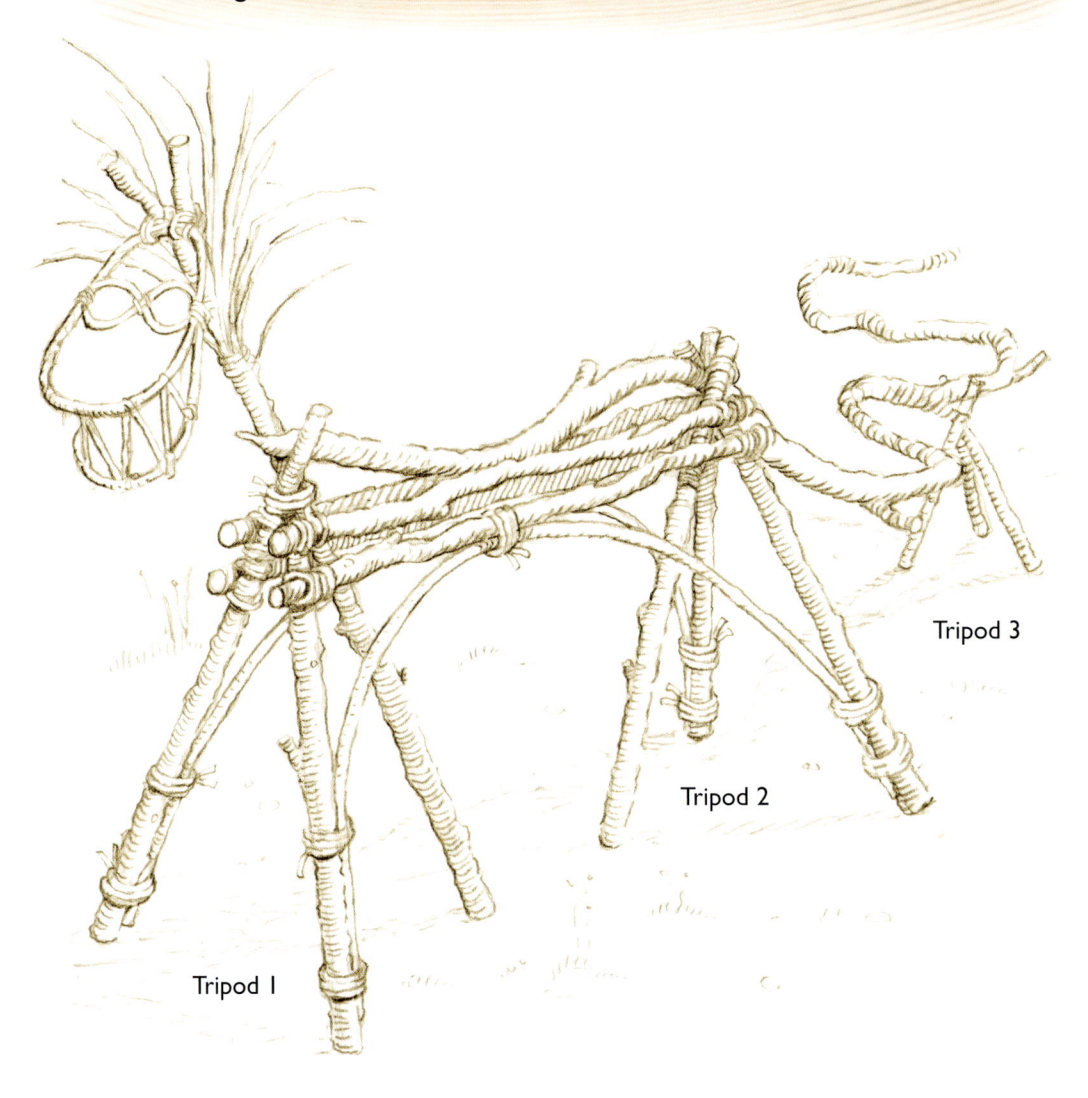

Tripod 3

Tripod 2

Tripod 1

The triangle

The triangle is a very good example of a basic building block from which many other possibilities can develop. By far the best idea is to make several triangles and then give children the freedom to come up with their own games and structures using one or several triangles joined together.

On the following pages are some suggestions.

Making a triangle

Some wonderful structures can be made by joining several triangular structures together, but a single frame can be used to define an area on the ground for the investigation of mini beasts and plants, or to use as a 'goal' in throwing games.

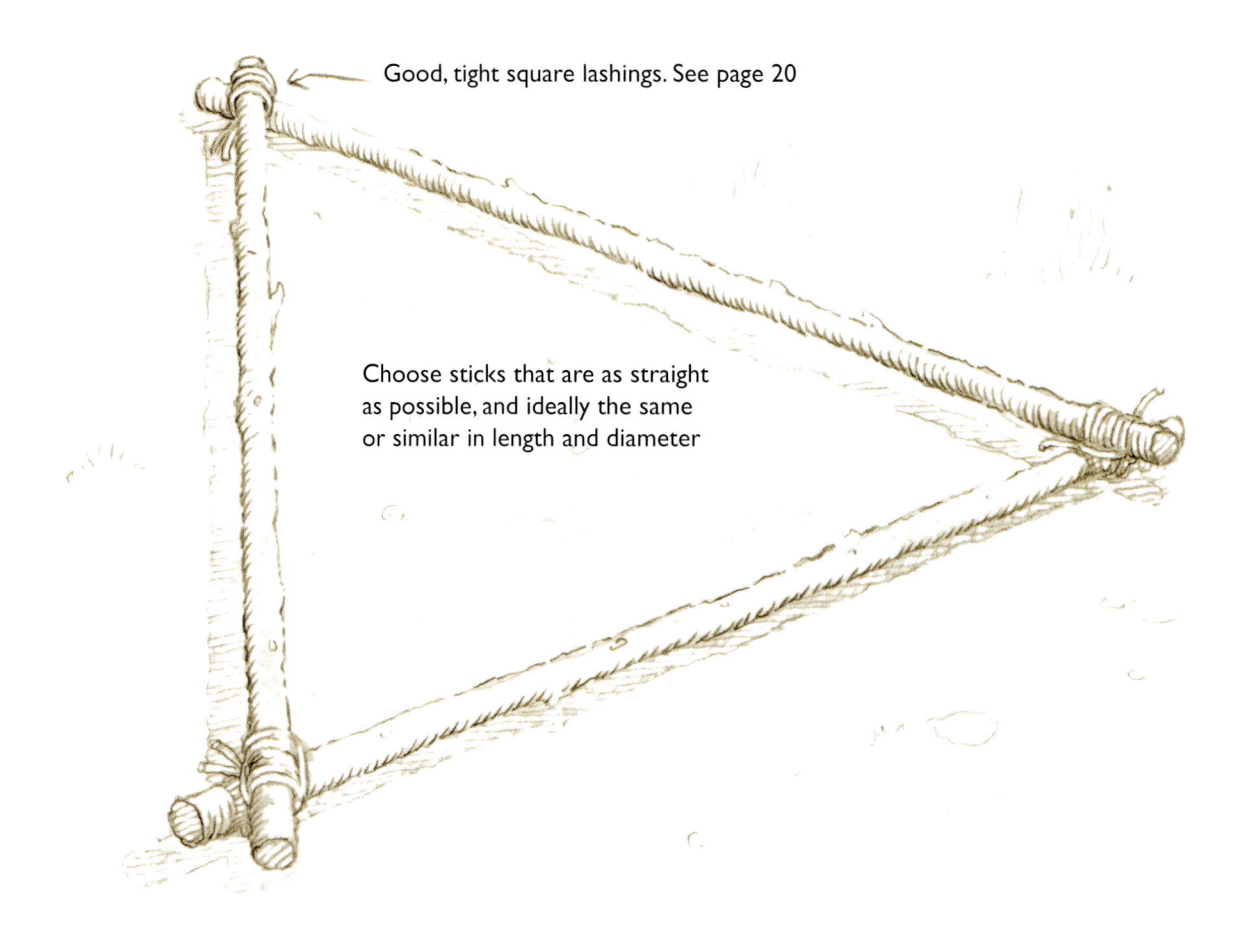

Good, tight square lashings. See page 20

Choose sticks that are as straight as possible, and ideally the same or similar in length and diameter

Modular triangles

Once one triangle has been made, explore what interesting and varied shapes and structures can be invented by attaching multiple triangles together.

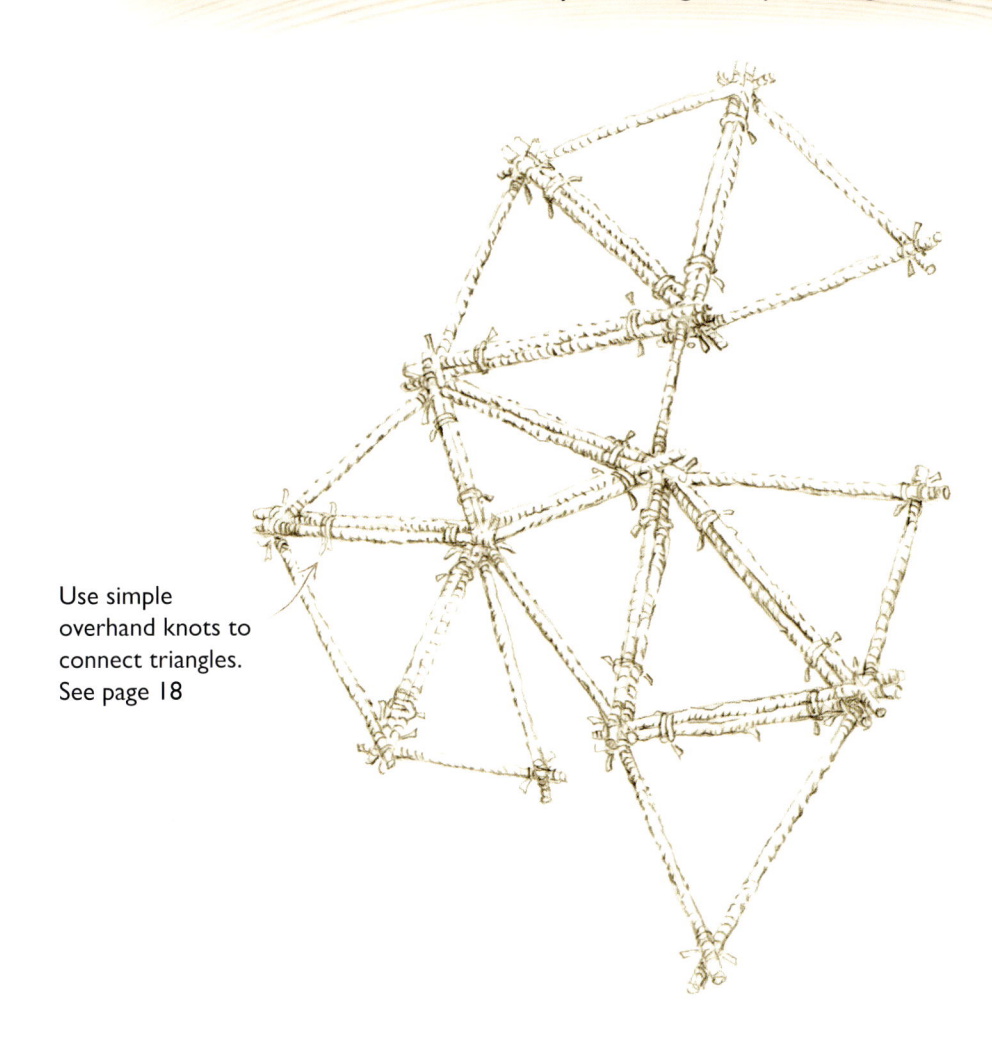

Use simple overhand knots to connect triangles. See page 18

Tetrahedron

A more solid structure than the tripod, the tetrahedron is a versatile structure that can be easily moved around without its shape being lost.

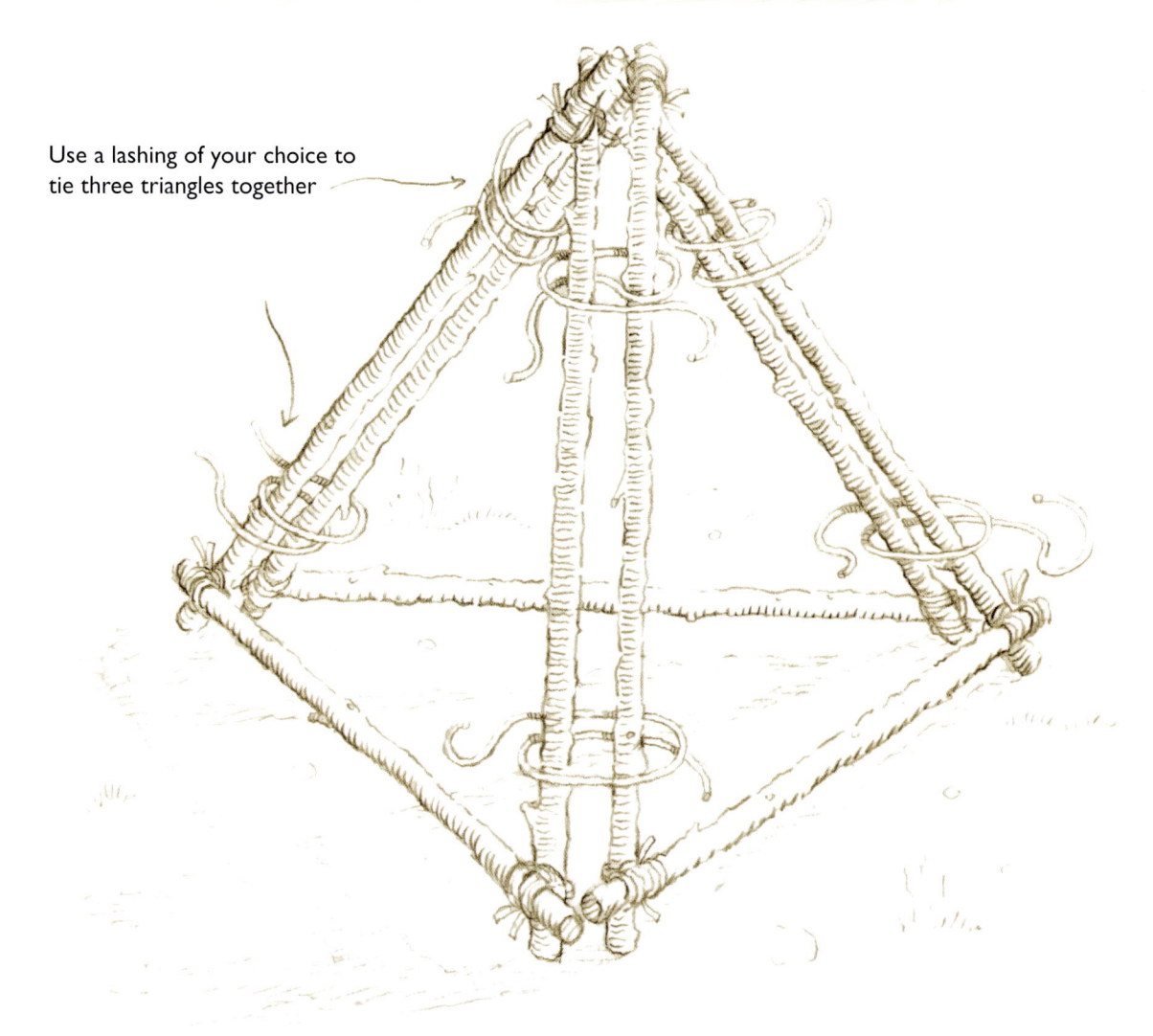

Use a lashing of your choice to tie three triangles together

Step ladder

Transform a tetrahedron into a stepladder, useful for reaching the roof of a bender (makeshift shelter), or a branch of a tree from which to hang things.

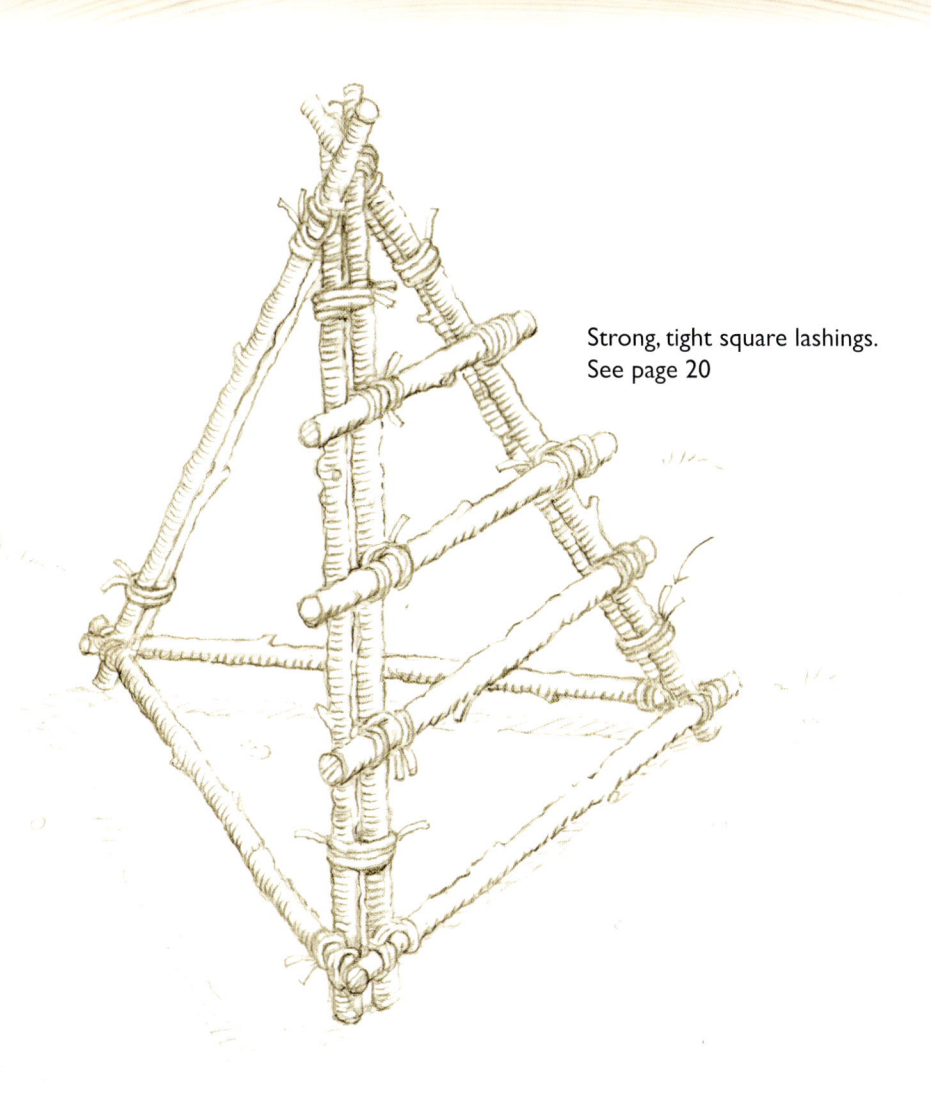

Strong, tight square lashings. See page 20

The triangle

Lantern

This lantern is made from a small tetrahedron constructed in a slightly different way. It is made by joining a triangle and mini tripod together.

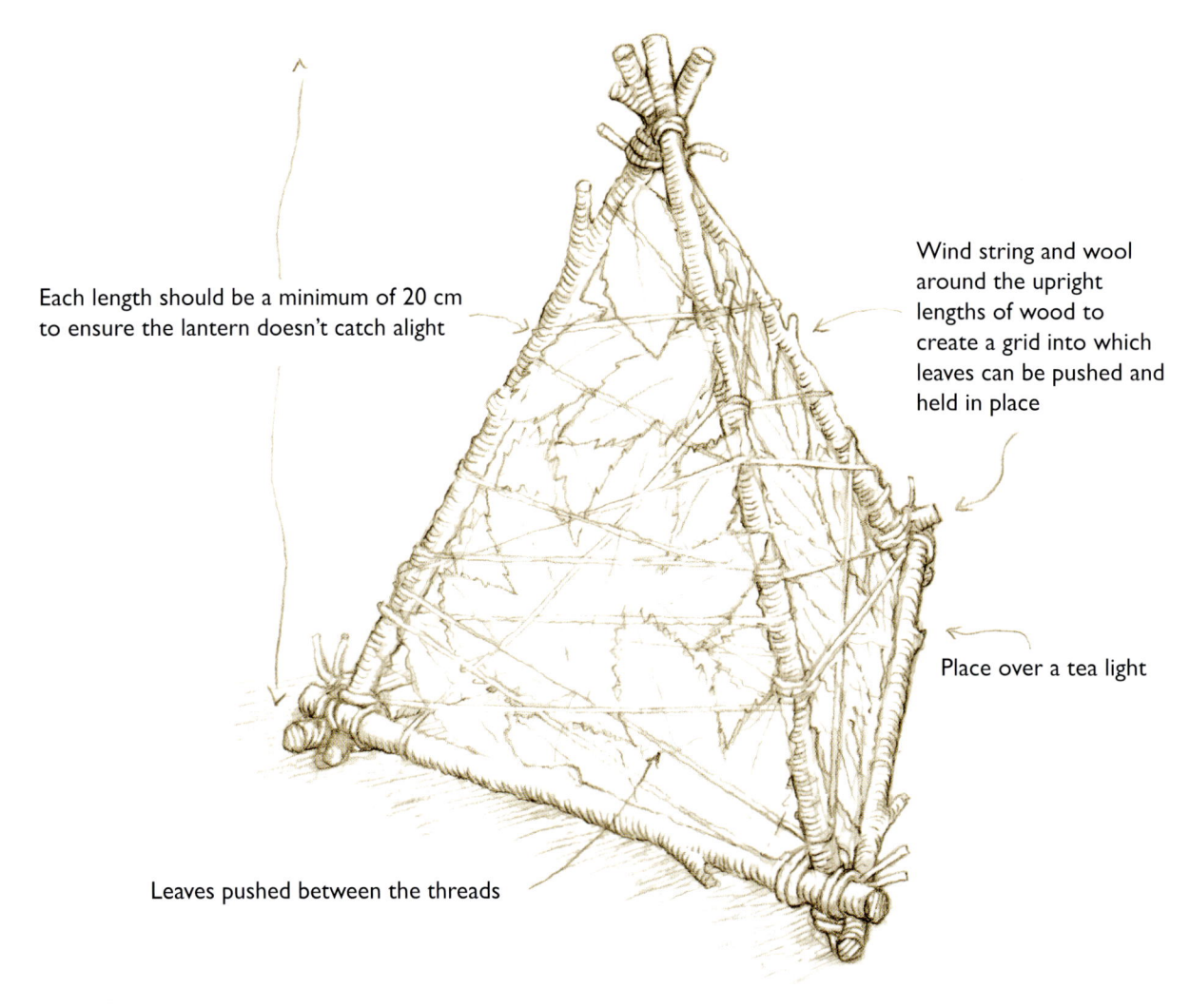

Each length should be a minimum of 20 cm to ensure the lantern doesn't catch alight

Wind string and wool around the upright lengths of wood to create a grid into which leaves can be pushed and held in place

Place over a tea light

Leaves pushed between the threads

Fixing a tea light inside your lantern

You will need three green sticks (hazel, willow or ash are ideal).

1 With a knife, cut a slit all the way through all the sticks

And make a point at one end

2 Push the pointed end through the slits…

3 …to make this structure

4 Tie it inside the lantern with a small jar wedged into it

Place a tea light inside the jar

The triangle 65

Using elder and willow

The following pages will give you some examples of what can be done with elder and willow. Use these ideas as a foundation for your own.

Set free your imagination…

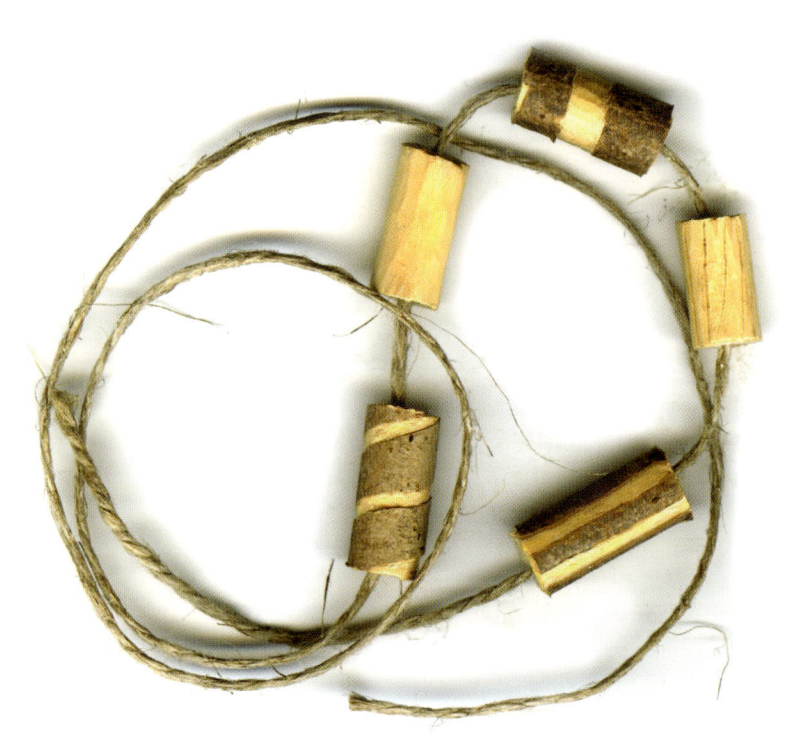

Blow pipe

Cut a length of elder, ensuring that there is a fair amount of pith to work with and a reasonable amount of wood surrounding it. If the wood is too thin and green the blow pipe will be too flimsy, and if the hole in the centre carrying the pith is too small it will be difficult to work with.

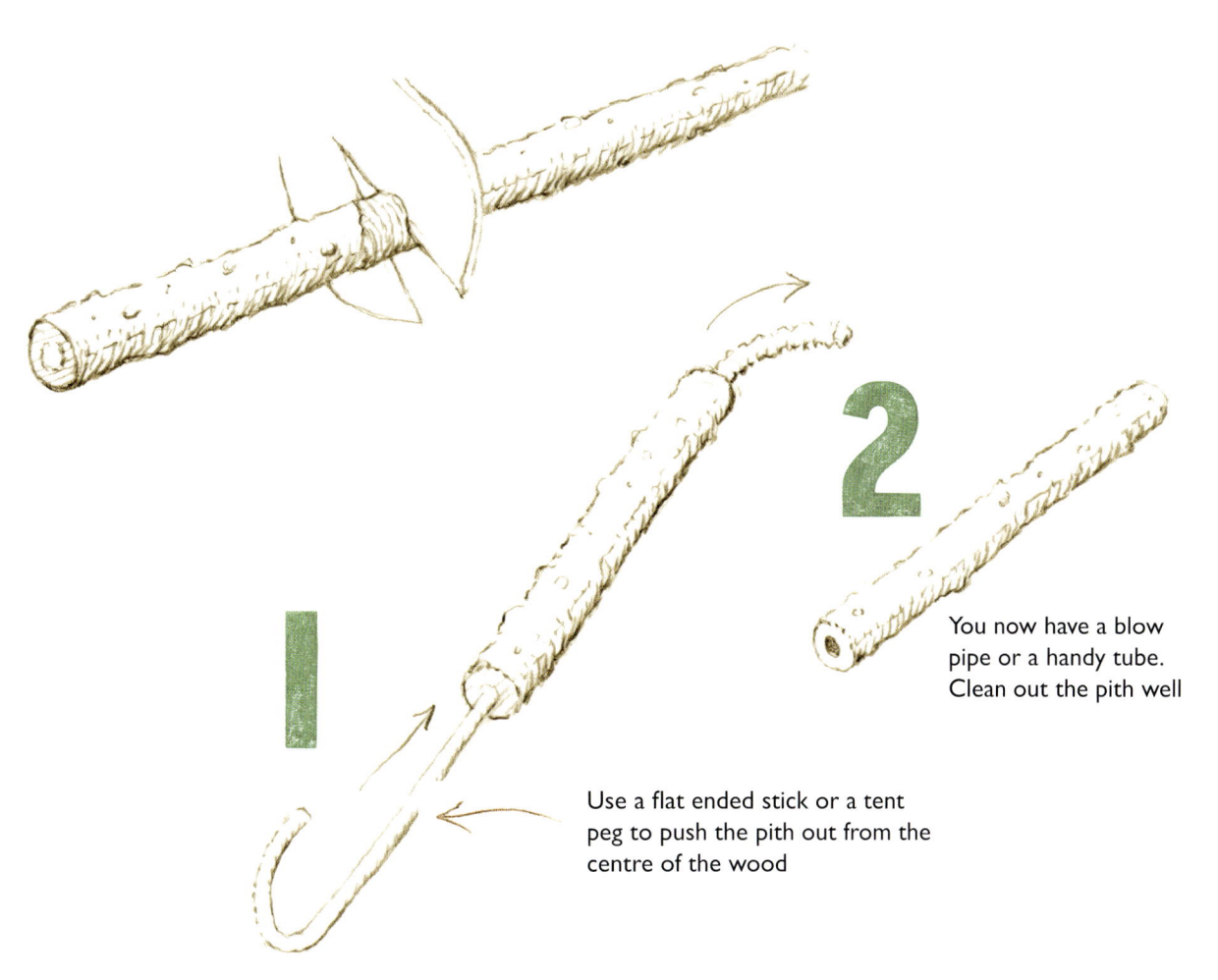

2

You now have a blow pipe or a handy tube. Clean out the pith well

1

Use a flat ended stick or a tent peg to push the pith out from the centre of the wood

Using elder and willow

There are lots of fun games to play with a blow pipe, such as 'Forest Subbuteo'. Use acorns or stones as your football

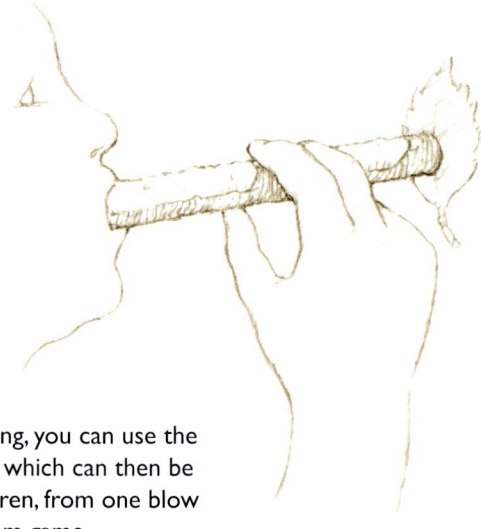

By sucking instead of blowing, you can use the blow pipe to pick up a leaf, which can then be passed down a line of children, from one blow pipe to another. A great team game

68   Using elder and willow

Elder beads

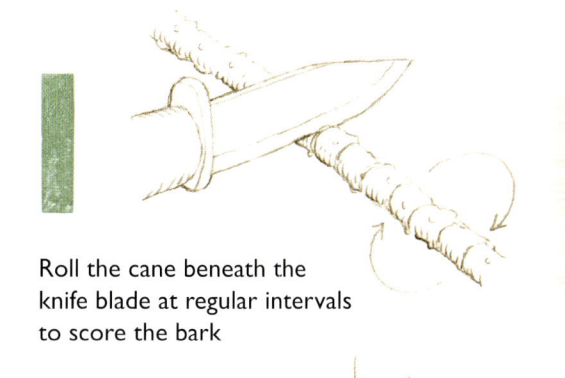

1 Roll the cane beneath the knife blade at regular intervals to score the bark

Elder beads can be used to make wonderful friendship bracelets or bead strings to hang from windows, light shades, trees and den roofs.

You can make various sizes of beads from different lengths of elder.

2 Use the end of a knife to tease out bark from every other section of scored bark

3 It is easier to carve designs on to the face of the length of cane before cutting it into individual beads

Ejected pith

Elder

Use a tent peg or flat ended stick to push out the pith of the cane

4 Try out a variety of different bead designs

Hoops

With bark

Spirals

Without bark

Using elder and willow 69

Forest rosaries

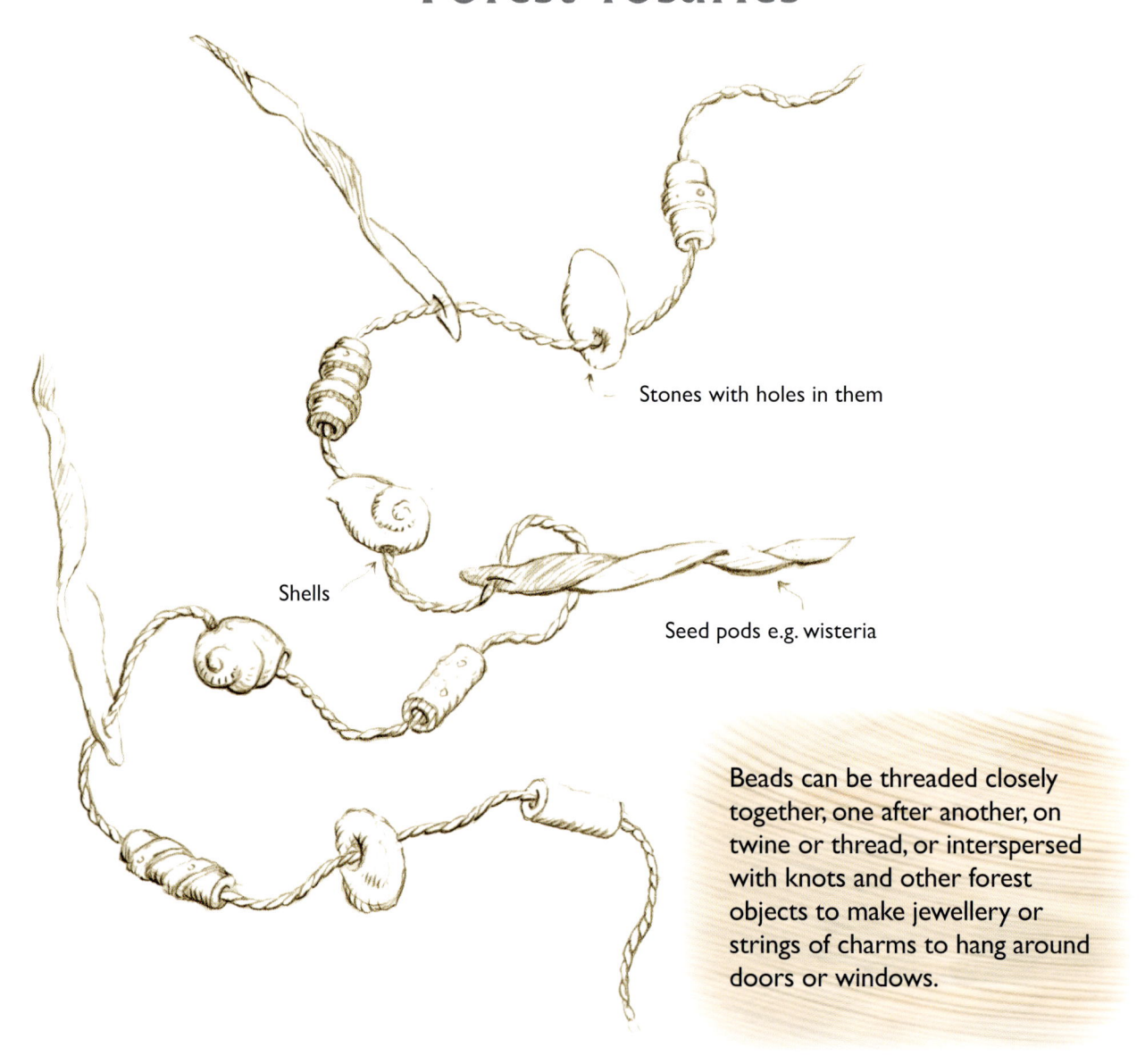

Stones with holes in them

Shells

Seed pods e.g. wisteria

Beads can be threaded closely together, one after another, on twine or thread, or interspersed with knots and other forest objects to make jewellery or strings of charms to hang around doors or windows.

Preparing willow cordage

Ribbons of bark stripped from willow can be plaited and woven together to make jewellery.

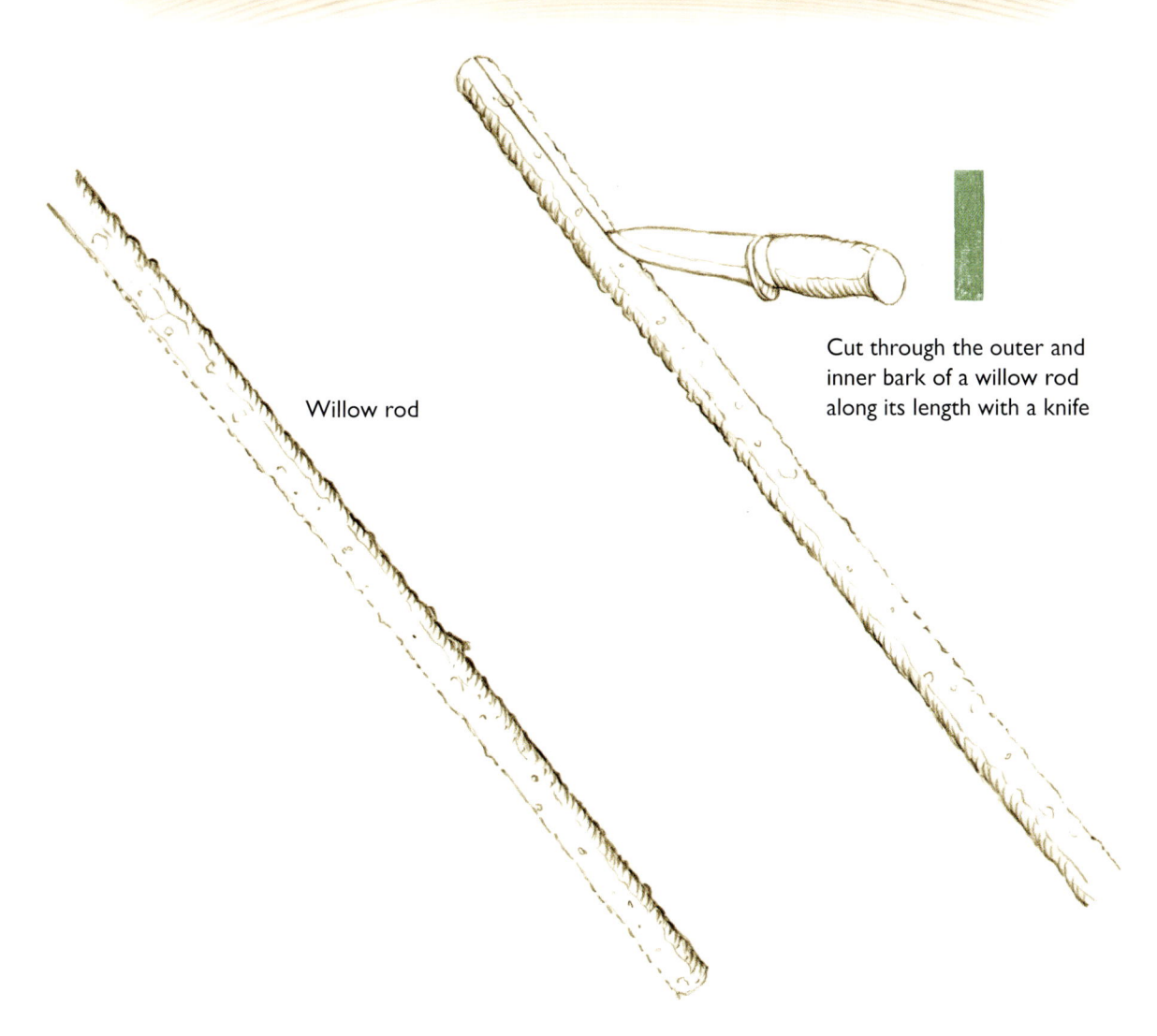

Willow rod

Cut through the outer and inner bark of a willow rod along its length with a knife

Using elder and willow

3 Carefully tear narrow ribbons of bark

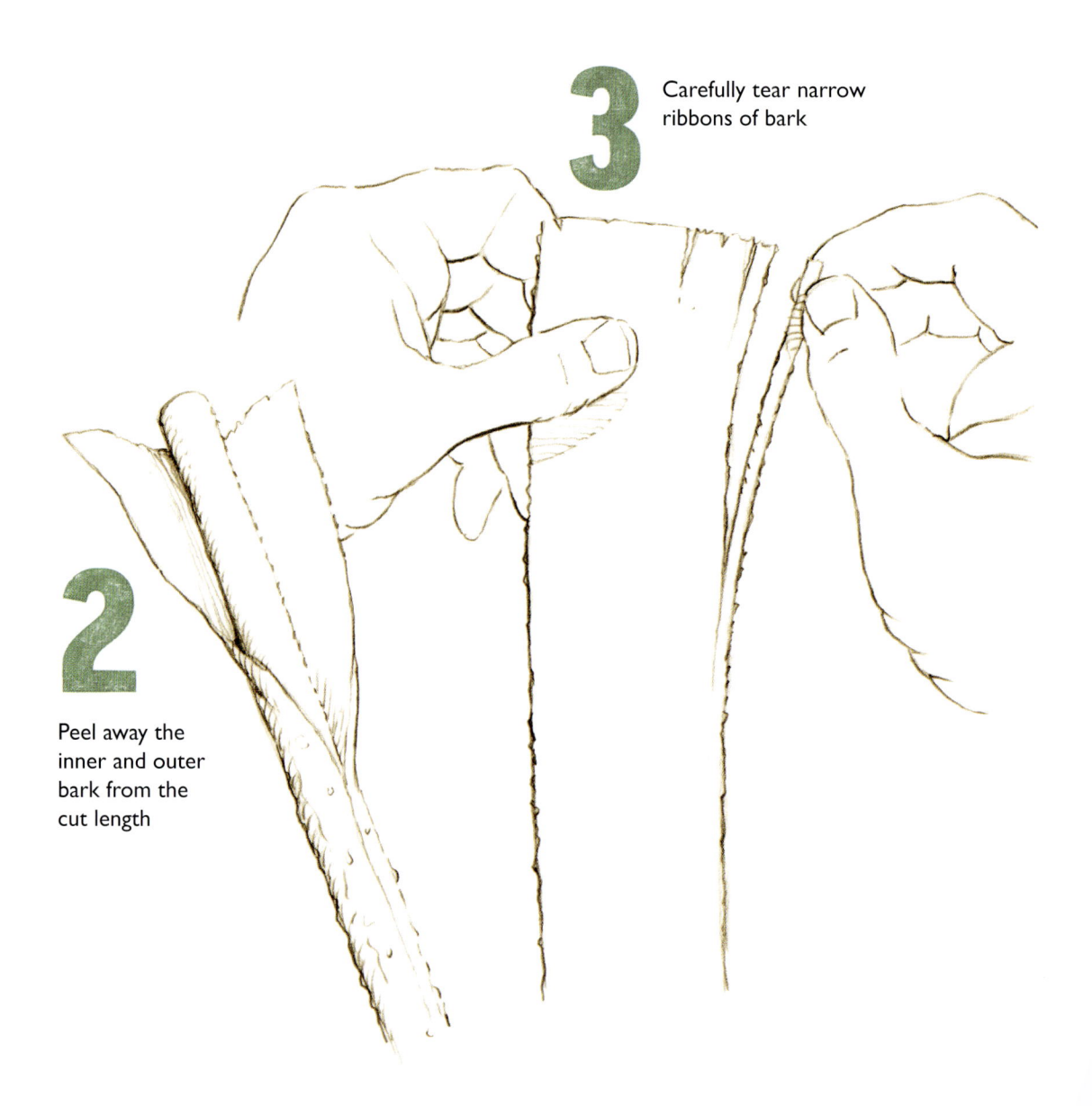

2 Peel away the inner and outer bark from the cut length

4

Take two ribbons. Fold one of them in half. Hold the folded length and the unfolded length side by side

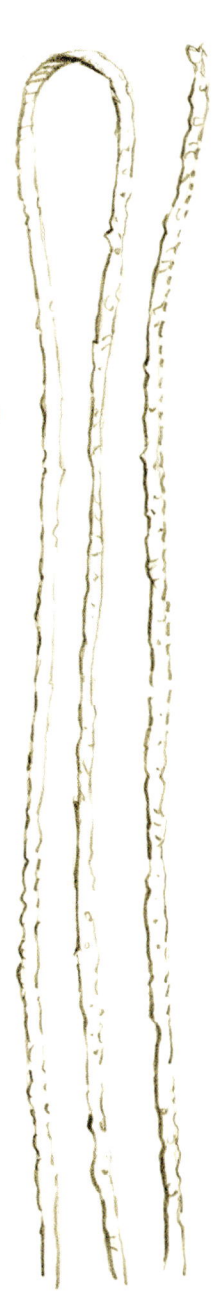

5

Tie an overhand knot. See page 18

Using elder and willow 73

Macramé bracelet 1

1

Using the willow cordage just shown.

To plait the ribbons of bark, simply alternate bringing the right hand side ribbon over the central ribbon, and then the left hand ribbon over the central ribbon where it folds

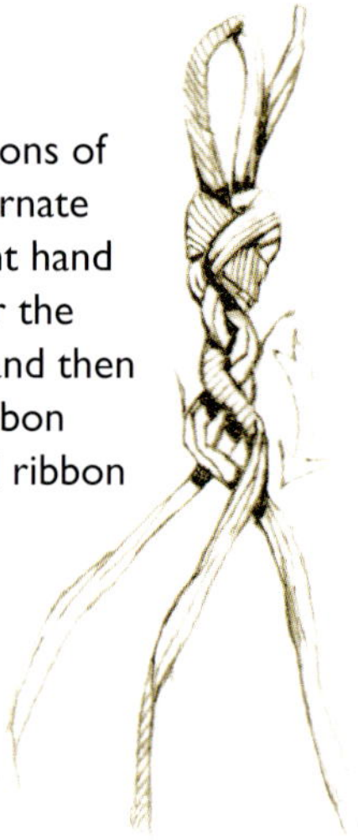

2

3

4

5 Tie a simple knot at the end of the bracelet

Thread elder bead

74 Using elder and willow

Macramé bracelet 2

These are shown using cord. But willow cordage could be used as an alternative. Take a metre length and start about a third of the way along it.

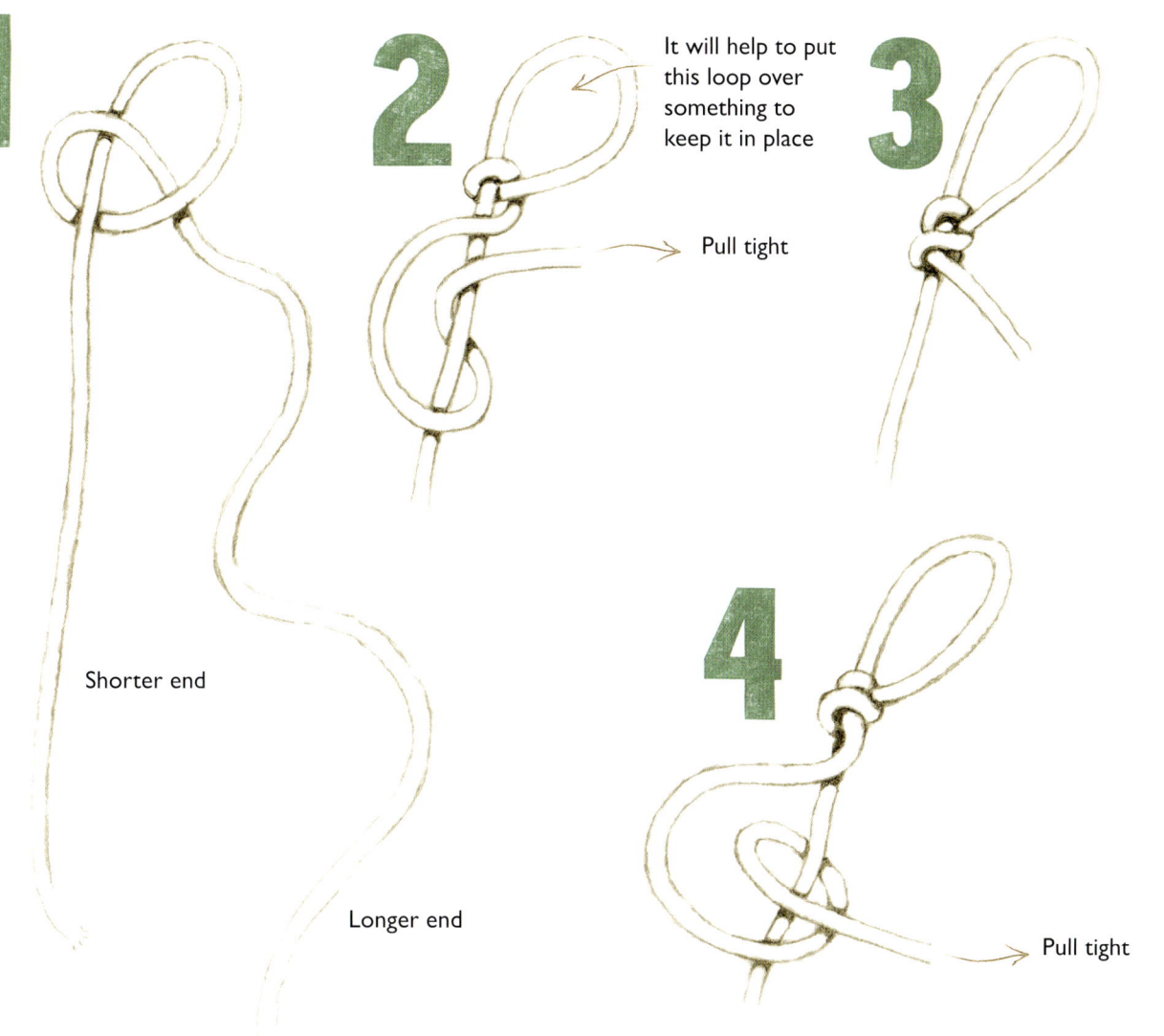

1

Shorter end

Longer end

2

It will help to put this loop over something to keep it in place

→ Pull tight

3

4

→ Pull tight

Using elder and willow 75

5 Repeat this knot over and over again to create a decorative effect

6 Thread beads at various points then carry on tying knots

Tie off end using an overhand knot. See page 18

76 Using elder and willow

Macramé bracelet 3

Use two separate lengths of cord to make this bracelet. One should measure about 50 cms, and the other should be roughly twice the length, measuring about a metre.

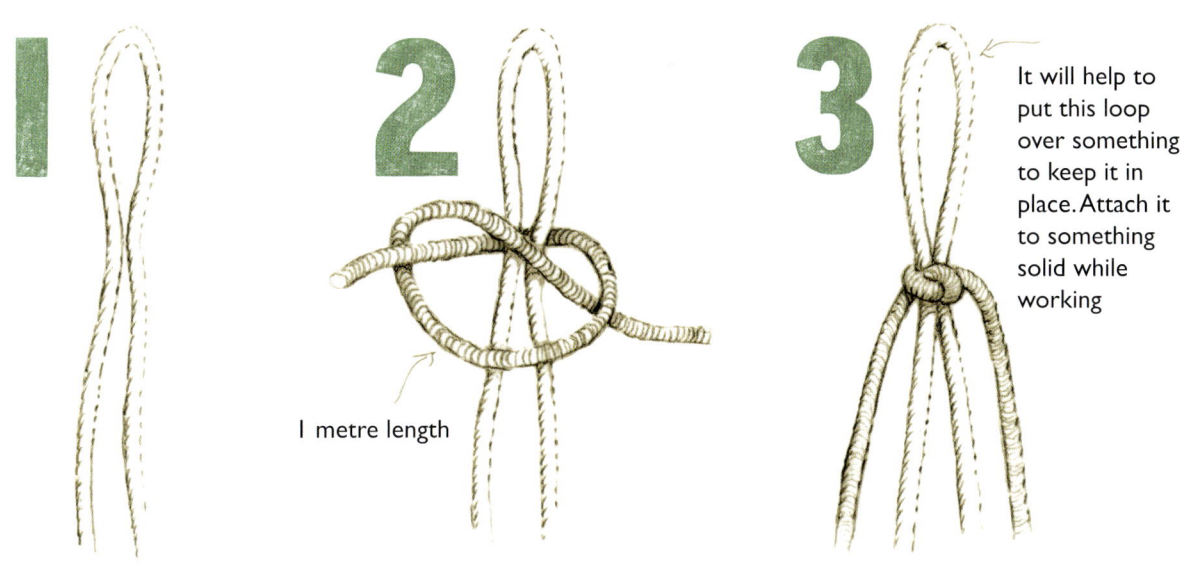

1 50 cm length

2 1 metre length

3 It will help to put this loop over something to keep it in place. Attach it to something solid while working

Using elder and willow

4

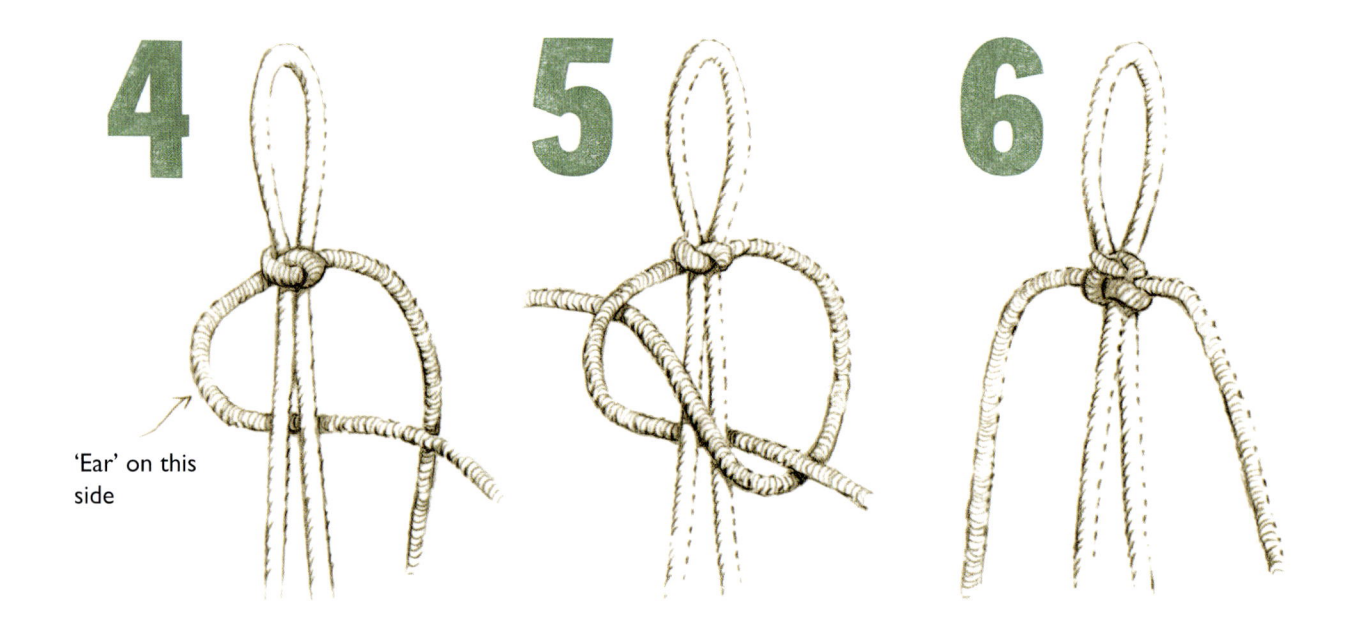

'Ear' on this side

5

6

7

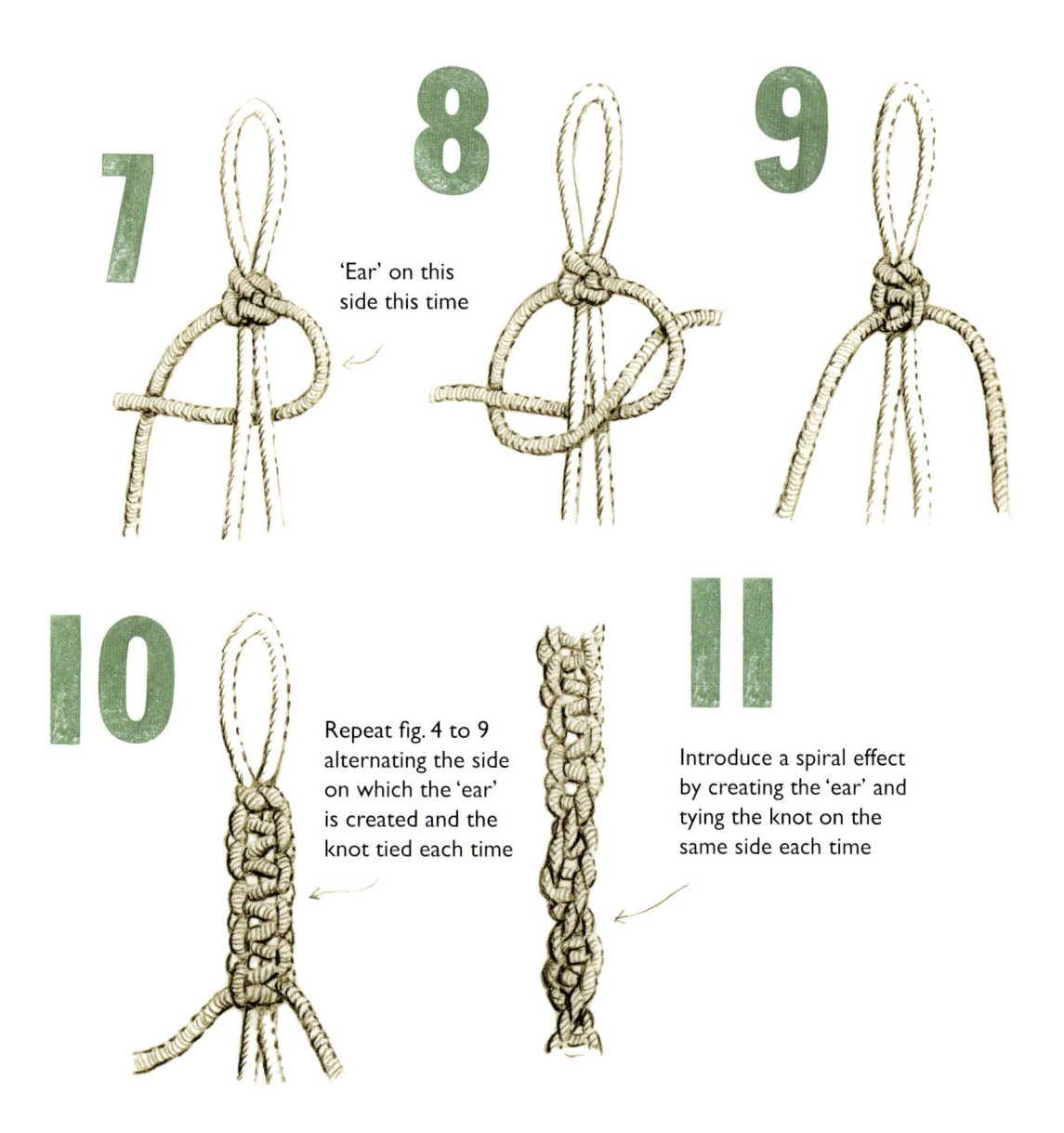

'Ear' on this side this time

8

9

10

Repeat fig. 4 to 9 alternating the side on which the 'ear' is created and the knot tied each time

11

Introduce a spiral effect by creating the 'ear' and tying the knot on the same side each time

Using elder and willow

Overhand knot

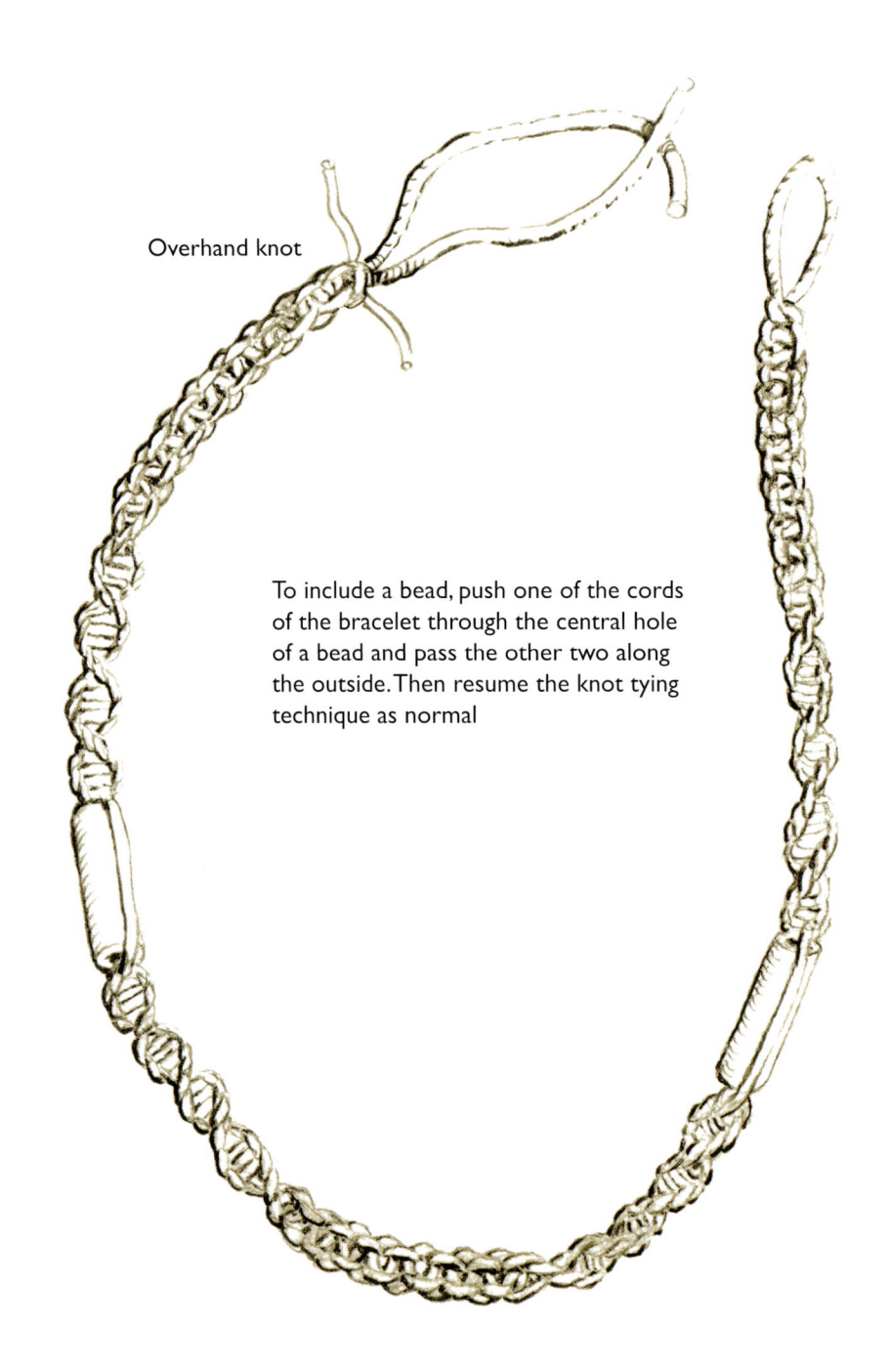

To include a bead, push one of the cords of the bracelet through the central hole of a bead and pass the other two along the outside. Then resume the knot tying technique as normal

Making puppets

These puppets look good when hung from trees. They are quick and easy to make, so ideal for miniature theatre productions.

Simple elder bead puppet

String elder beads on to three separate lengths of cord as shown.

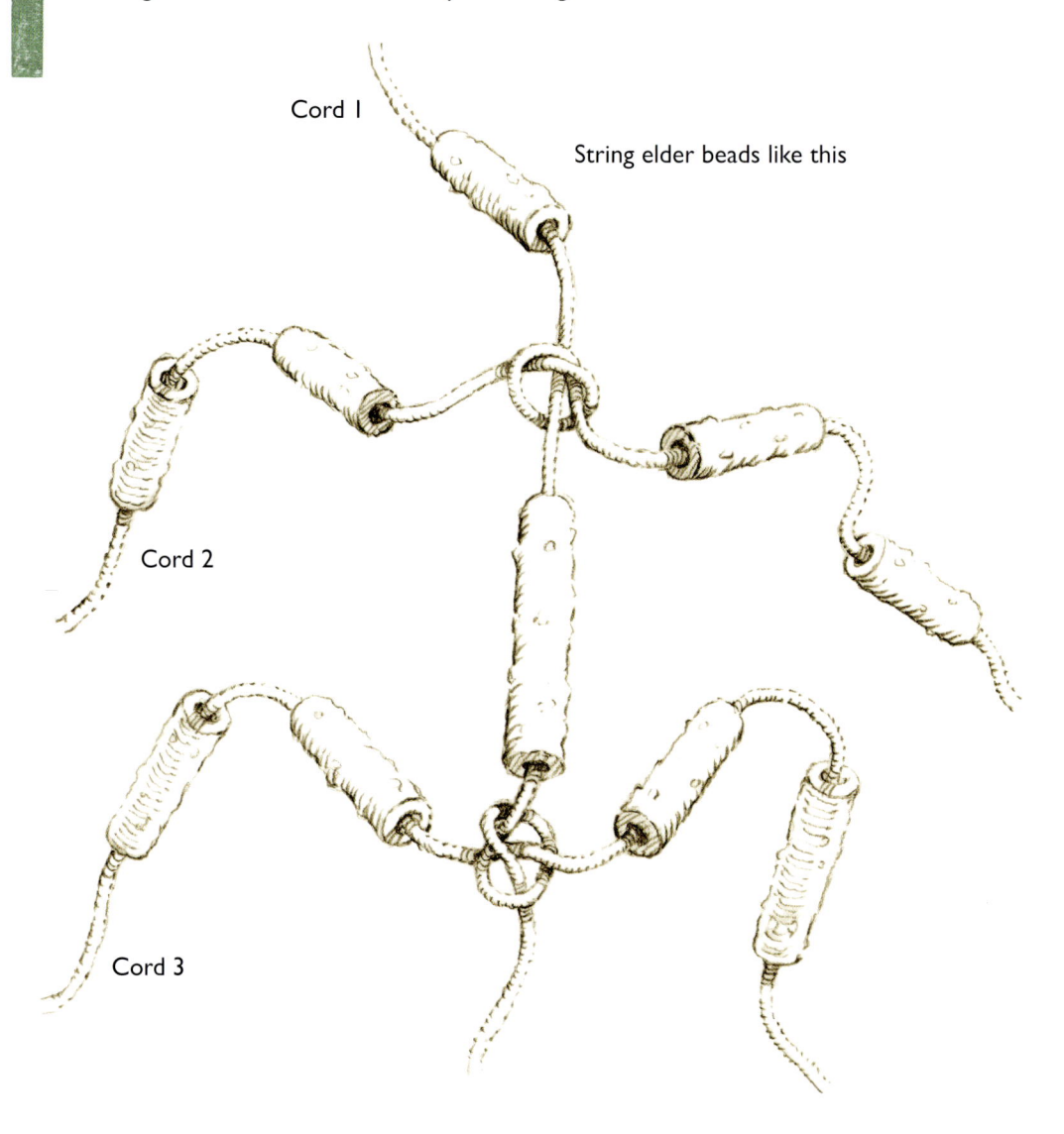

Cord 1

String elder beads like this

Cord 2

Cord 3

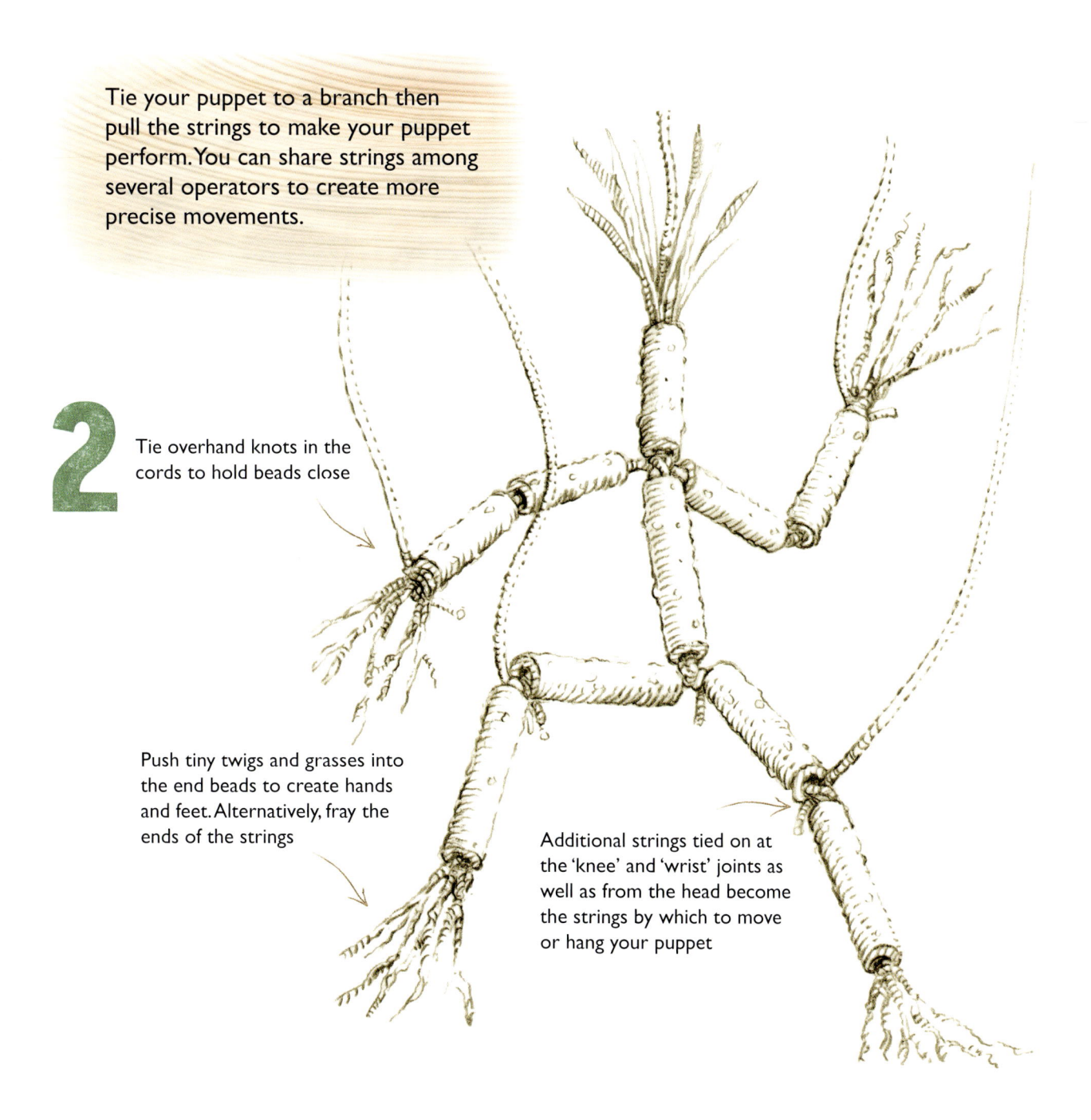

Tie your puppet to a branch then pull the strings to make your puppet perform. You can share strings among several operators to create more precise movements.

2

Tie overhand knots in the cords to hold beads close

Push tiny twigs and grasses into the end beads to create hands and feet. Alternatively, fray the ends of the strings

Additional strings tied on at the 'knee' and 'wrist' joints as well as from the head become the strings by which to move or hang your puppet

Making puppets

Horse puppet

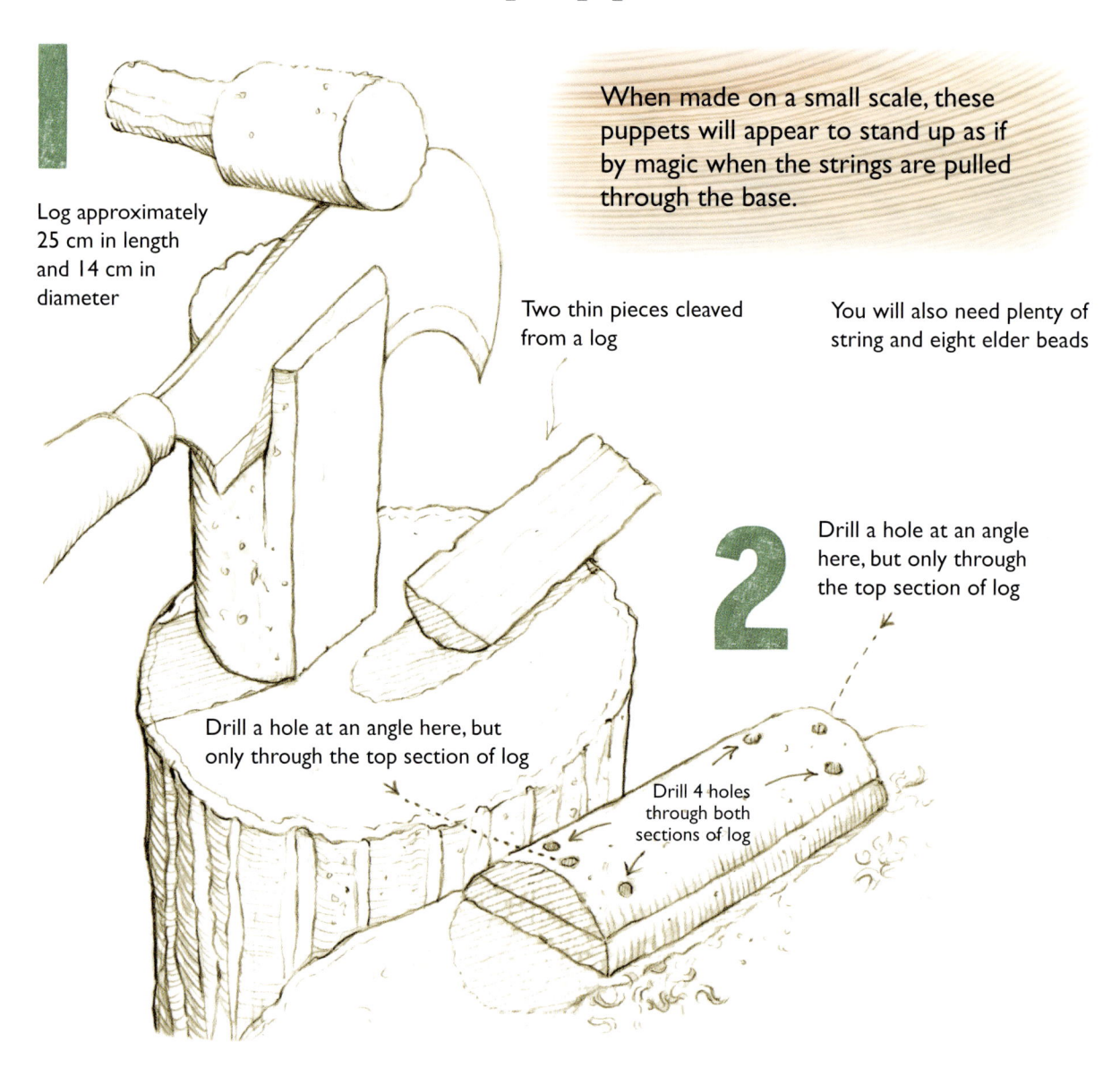

1 Log approximately 25 cm in length and 14 cm in diameter

When made on a small scale, these puppets will appear to stand up as if by magic when the strings are pulled through the base.

Two thin pieces cleaved from a log

You will also need plenty of string and eight elder beads

2 Drill a hole at an angle here, but only through the top section of log

Drill a hole at an angle here, but only through the top section of log

Drill 4 holes through both sections of log

84 Making puppets

3

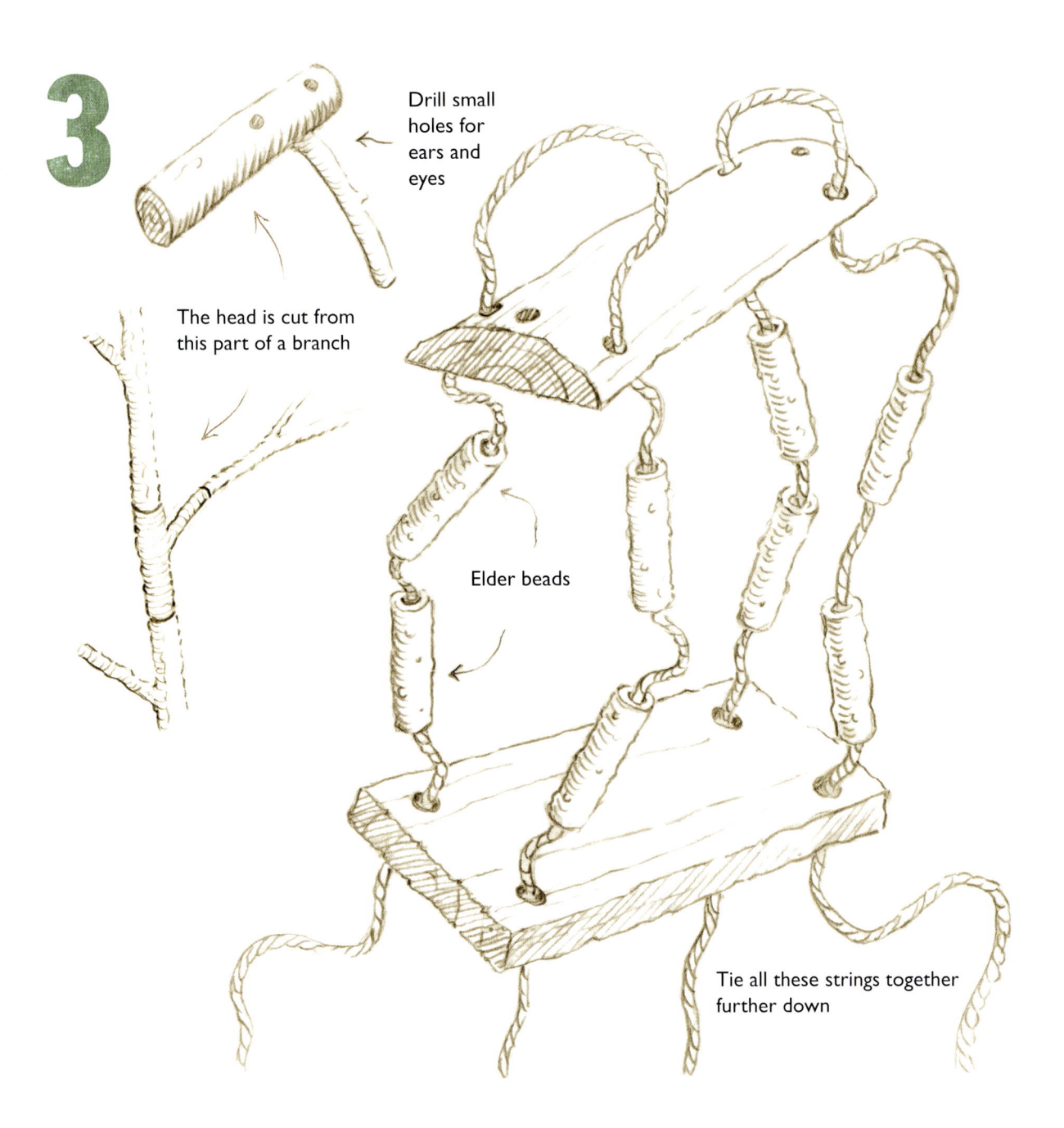

Drill small holes for ears and eyes

The head is cut from this part of a branch

Elder beads

Tie all these strings together further down

Making puppets 85

4

Add leaves, feathers, wool or grasses for ears and tail

Pull strings through base to make the horse stand up. Knots can be tied beneath the base to secure the horse in position

86 Making puppets

Man of the forest puppet

This is a more elaborate and much bigger version of the elder puppet. Here are all the bits and pieces you will need.

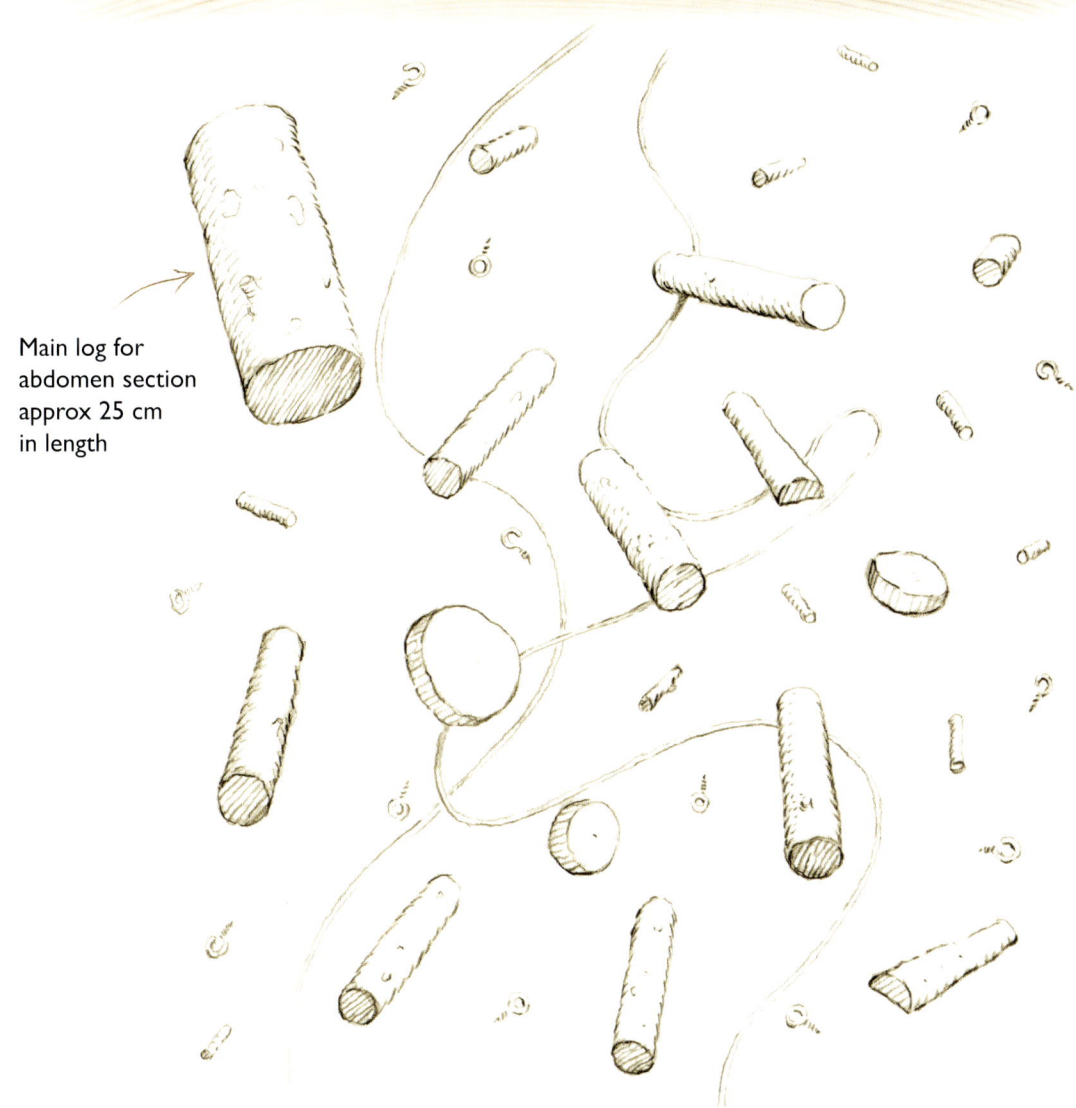

Main log for abdomen section approx 25 cm in length

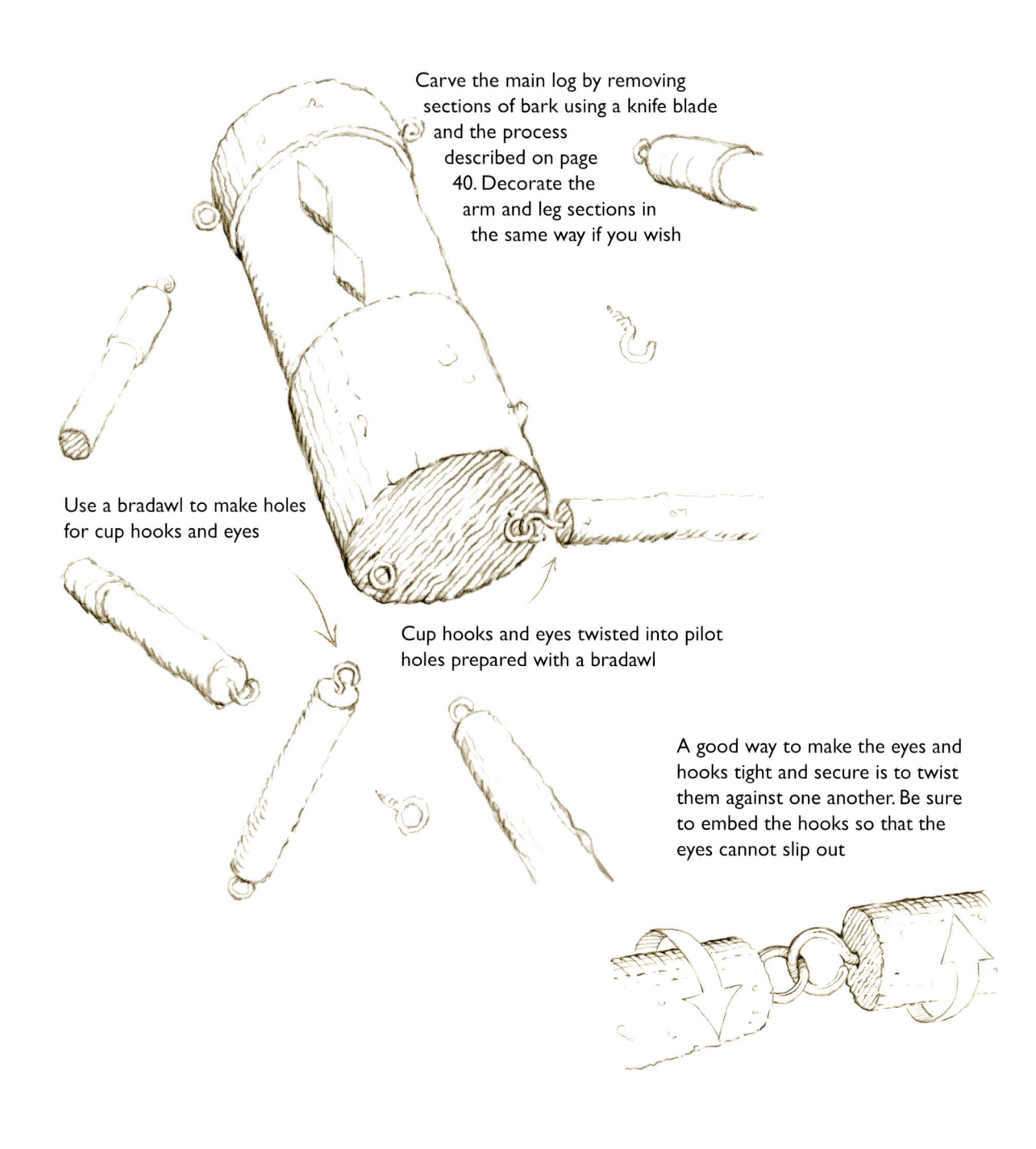

Carve the main log by removing sections of bark using a knife blade and the process described on page 40. Decorate the arm and leg sections in the same way if you wish

Use a bradawl to make holes for cup hooks and eyes

Cup hooks and eyes twisted into pilot holes prepared with a bradawl

A good way to make the eyes and hooks tight and secure is to twist them against one another. Be sure to embed the hooks so that the eyes cannot slip out

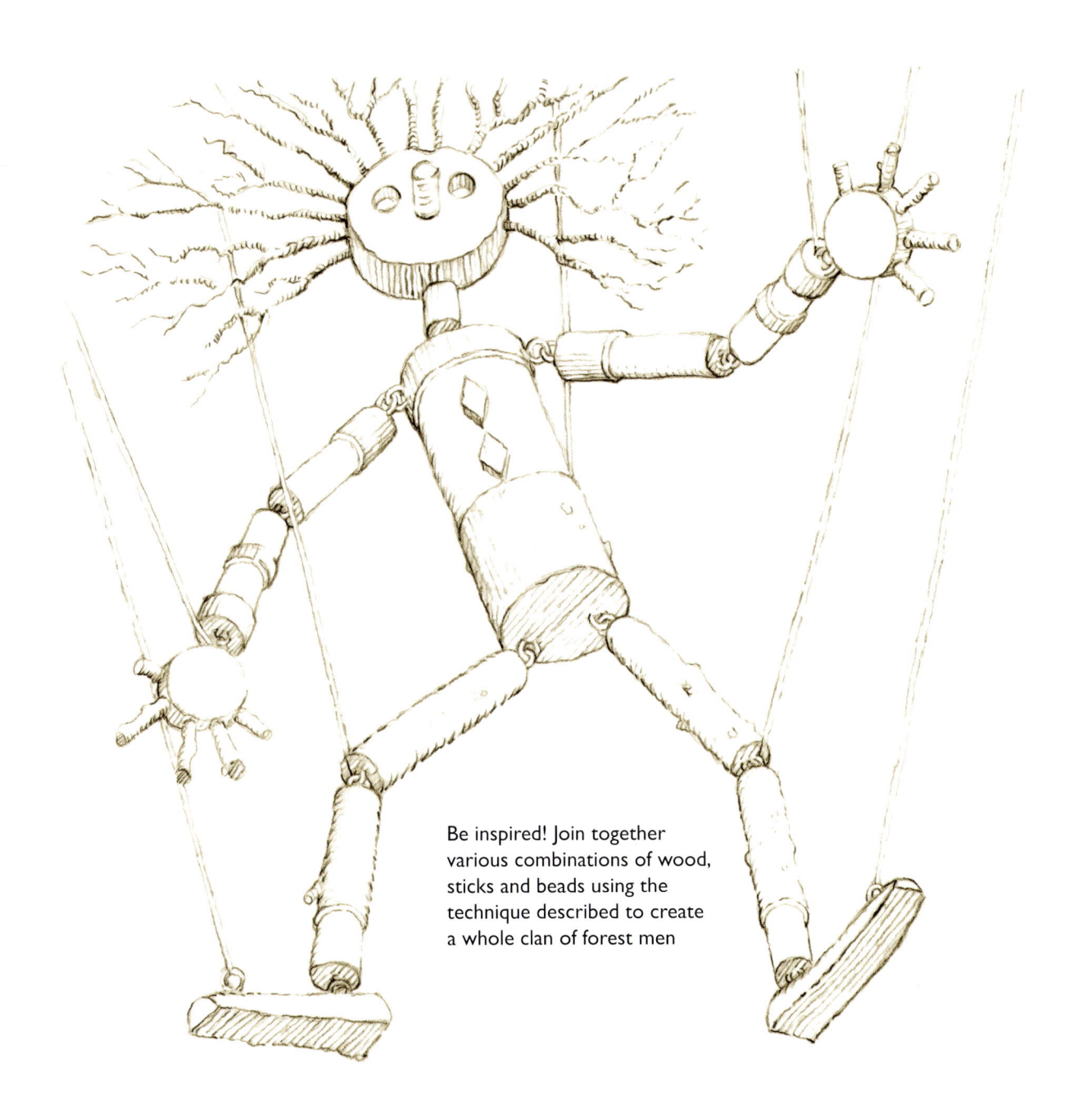

Be inspired! Join together various combinations of wood, sticks and beads using the technique described to create a whole clan of forest men

Making puppets 89

Giant puppets

The spaciousness of the woodlands makes
large-scale projects possible.
When working or playing outdoors, why
not take advantage of this unique facility to
extend the boundaries of your imagination?
These large-scale puppets can be made from
long rods of 'green' bendy wood, or lengths
and chunks of dead wood lashed
or tied at the joints.

Giant horse puppet

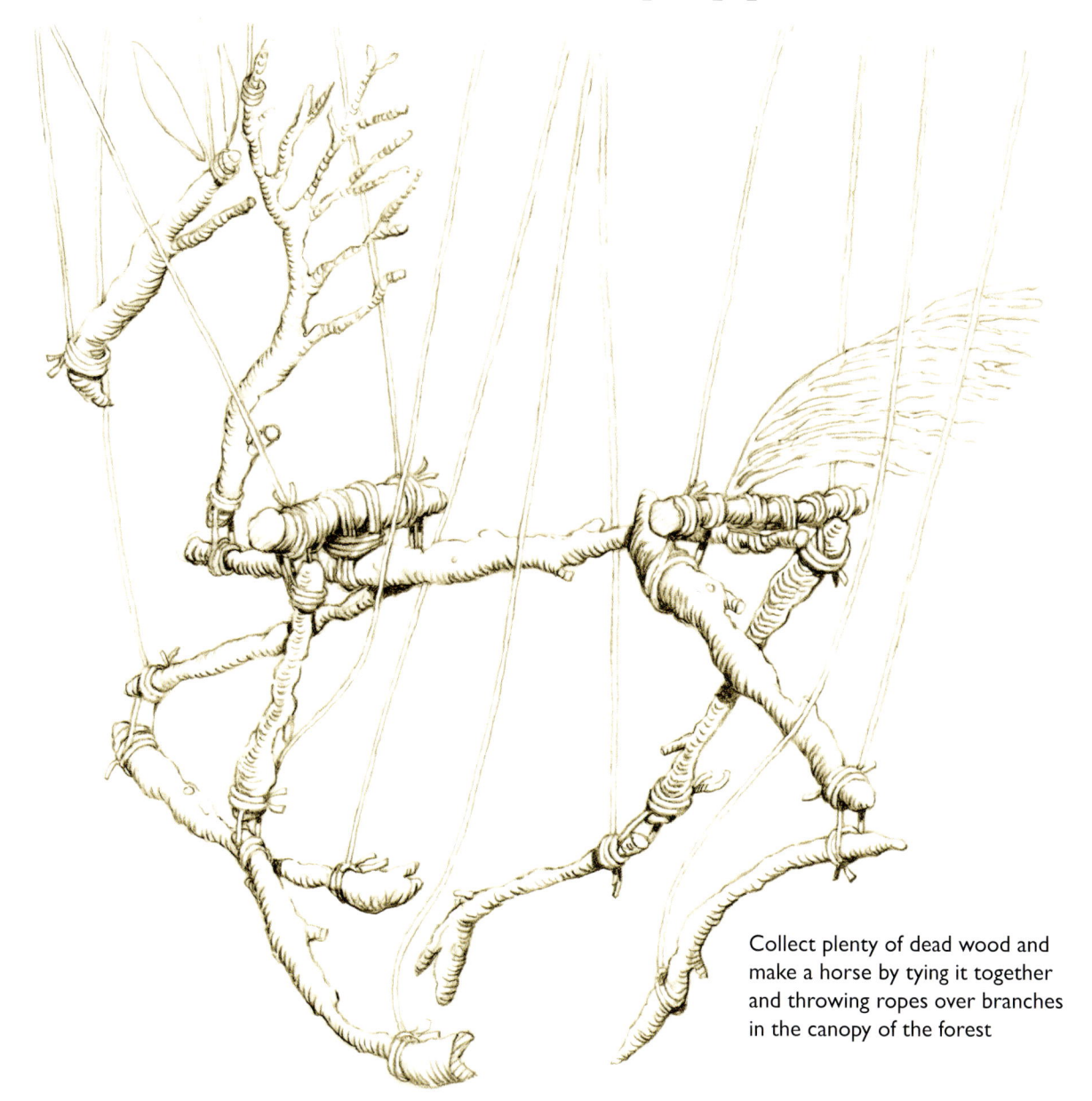

Collect plenty of dead wood and make a horse by tying it together and throwing ropes over branches in the canopy of the forest

Giant dragon puppet

Try out using different ways to tie the giant puppet together, such as a combination using cup hooks

Afterword

Woods and wood culture are a fundamental part of our existence. This delightful and very accessible book is a true reflection of our wood culture. Patrick's beautiful sketches and very clear instructions in some basic woodcraft techniques for making wood 'stuff' will guarantee to deepen anyone's connection with woods and the crafts associated with them. This book provides a great starting point for people wishing to work with woodcrafts using a few basic tools and tricks of the trade. As Patrick explains in his introduction, this can be a truly deeply meditative and connecting experience.

In my many years involved with woodland and environmental education I have often heard the mantra from teachers and students alike… 'Oh I'm not creative!' What this book does is demystify woodcrafts and give some very simple and well illustrated foundations for enabling educators, parents and children to find their own creativity. The knots and basic tool techniques, clearly and simply explained, along with basic structures such as ladders, nets and triangles, show how these can provide the basis for more complicated and creative structures such as stargazing chairs. Once you have mastered the basic techniques shown in the book, you are guaranteed to enter a whole new creative world that these foundations can support.

In recent years there has been a growth in woodland education, both formal and informal, supporting those involved with education to gain more confidence in getting into the trees. This growth has been facilitated through organisations like the Forestry Commission's education projects such as the Forest Education Initiative, the Forest Education Network, The Woodland Trust, The Small Woods Association, The Sylva Foundation and the many organisations involved with Forest School – the Forest School Association and the many Forest School training providers and delivery organisations. There are at least 10,000 trained Forest School leaders in the UK, and countless other educators, teachers and parents who take children, young adults and adults alike into the woods on a less regular basis.

Our woodlands have come and gone over the thousands of years since the last ice age. Recent and current threats have included lack of management and increase in global trade and diseases, the latest being ash dieback. If we are to both conserve and increase these important 'breathing spaces' for all, humans and non-humans alike, then we need to connect more people with our woodland heritage and see woods as places for living and learning. Questions such as what woods feel like, what they are used for, how to sustain them and how they support us every second of our life are answered through experiences such as those espoused by Patrick. More importantly, just being in woods working with handcrafts and telling stories while whittling away can go really deep and hopefully engender a 'cherishing' attitude to the natural world. Woodlands have been a fabric of our existence in the UK ever since Neanderthal man walked and indeed swung through the trees. As Colin Tudge said, in his book *The Secret Life of Trees*, 'We have left our first ancestors far behind but we are creatures of the forest still.'

This is a real 'woodland companion' and will, I guarantee, increase any learner's enjoyment, understanding and 'feeling' for our woods and woodcrafts. Happy 'crafting and creating'!

Jon Cree
Founding Chair of the Forest School Association.
Ecological educator and trainer, and Grandpappy!
Co-editor of *Storytelling for Nature Connection: Environment, community and story-based learning*.
Co-author of the highly acclaimed *The Essential Guide to Forest School and Nature Pedagogy* (Routledge, 2021).

Other Books from Hawthorn Press

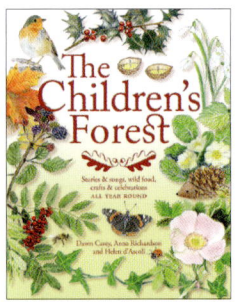

The Children's Forest
Dawn Casey, Anna Richardson, Helen d'Ascoli

A rich and abundant treasury in celebration of the outdoors, this book encourages children's natural fascination with the forest and its inhabitants. An enchanting book where imagination, story and play bring alive the world of the forest. Full of games, facts, celebrations, craft activities, recipes, foraging, stories and Forest School skills. Ideal for ages 5–12 it will be enjoyed by all ages.
336pp; 250 x 200mm; paperback; ISBN: 978-1-907359-91-0

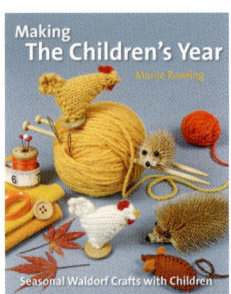

Making the Children's Year
Seasonal Waldorf Crafts with Children
Marije Rowling

Drawing on the creative ethos of Steiner Waldorf education, this is a full-colour second edition of *The Children's Year*. Packed with all kinds of seasonal crafts, for beginners and experienced crafters, this book is a gift for parents seeking to make toys that will inspire children and provide an alternative to throwaway culture.
240pp; 250 x 200mm; paperback; ISBN: 978-1-907359-69-9

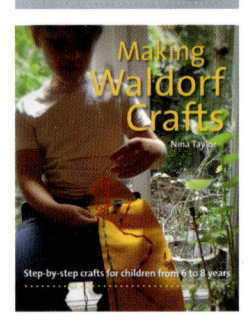

Making Waldorf Crafts
Step-by-step crafts for children from 6 to 8 years
Nina Taylor

Practical craft projects suitable for children aged 6–8 years, classes 1 and 2 of Steiner-Waldorf school to follow on their own or with support. Techniques include spinning, knitting, sewing and weaving and the projects and techniques are accompanied by stories and anecdotes with a narrative that children won't be able to resist.
128pp; 250 x 200mm; paperback; ISBN: 978-1-912480-39-5

Ordering books

If you have difficulties ordering Hawthorn Press books from a bookshop you can order direct from our website **www.hawthornpress.com** or from our UK distributor:
BookSource, 50 Cambuslang Road, Glasgow, G32 8NB
Tel: (0845) 370 0067, Email: orders@booksource.net.
Details of our overseas distributors can be found on our website.

Hawthorn Press
www.hawthornpress.com